SOCIAL WEALTH

{ How to Build Extraordinary
RELATIONSHIPS
by Transforming the Way We
Live, Love, Lead and Network }

JASON TREU

Social Wealth

Copyright © 2017 by Be Extraordinary, LLC

ISBN-10: 0-692-85015-5
ISBN-13: 978-0-692-85015-2

Cover artist: Derek Murphy (www.creativindiecovers.com)
Editor: Lindsey Alexander (lindsey-alexander.com)

DEDICATION

Your life experience comes down to two things: the quality of your relationships with yourself and other people, and what you create and collaborate with others. No one does it alone, but you have to start with yourself.

Take the time and effort to invest in both these relationships to:

- Open up limitless amounts of love, peace, excitement, and fulfillment
- Test your limits to create the best "you"
- Explore your curiosities and passions
- Turn dreams into reality for yourself and others (including financial ones)
- Create your own business or develop the career you love
- Live with authenticity and vulnerability, and move beyond shame
- Give, help and inspire all those you touch
- Be a leader that people admire, respect, like and believe in whole heartedly
- Develop meaningful connections and create true belonging

I dedicate this book to all the people I have met already and all those I will be meeting. I can't wait to meet you all to create successes, learn from failures, celebrate the small daily victories, laugh until our stomachs hurt, create deep and meaningful relationships, and help, give, inspire, network and lead along the way.

I look forward to serving you in any way I can, and going on this life journey together...*because it's better together.* Let's make it happen...starting NOW!

CONTENTS

Attention Purchasers of My Bestselling Book "Social Wealth"

**As a purchaser of my bestselling book, I want to do
something special for you. I want to gift you
my special report...**

*"15 Key Social Wealth Tools
To Accelerate Building Extraordinary Relationships"*
This report details the 15 ultra-useful social tools I use to
maintain and grow my local tribe of 15,000 and 30,000-strong
tribe of friends, business colleagues, clients, customers,
and acquaintances.

I wouldn't be where I am today without them.

My clients have used them to meet Richard Branson,
Bill Gates, Tim Cook, Peter Diamandis, Chris Anderson
(Owner of TED Conferences), Mark Cuban, and many,
many major influencers.

These tools make it easy, almost effortless.
And they're my gift to you for purchasing *Social Wealth*.

**Email me directly at Jason@jasontreu.com and
put in the Subject Line: Social Wealth Tools. I'll also send
you my audiobook for free as well.**

**PS: Be sure to check out JasonTreu.com for blogs, videos,
podcasts with experts, coaching, products, and more to
take your business, career, leadership and management
skills to the highest levels. I also will share strategies on
creating a high performing culture, hiring and retaining
"A+" employees, simplifying business processes, managing
others, dealing with workplace conflicts and much more.**

PREFACE

Appropriately enough, I was introduced to Jason Treu by a friend.

Jason had such a way about him. He was not just friendly. He was not just likeable.

Those qualities can, at times, be helpful but superficial. As a contrast, Jason wanted to really get to know ME.

Not to know me so he could take advantage of me. He wanted to know me so he could figure out how he could help ME!

Even though it was he who had come to me needing my help. I was impressed.

After spending an enormous amount of time collaborating with Jason, this is my personal assessment:

Jason's overarching strategy for networking and relationship building is identical to <u>Warren Buffet's approach to financial wealth building</u>.

Like Warren, Jason's mission is focusing on creating QUALITY relationships. He amasses LONG TERM social capital. Truth be told, I believe he places the value of relationships higher than any monetary gain he could ever generate.

I strongly suspect Jason's social bank account is bulging.

I've experienced his friendship firsthand. I've seen him light up when he talks about his clients and the people he meets at his charity events. I've seen him in action as he hits a big city, meeting personally with major influencers to promote a project he's involved with or to build a relationship after one of his speaking engagements. And he also does this across the world.

Of course, he leverages the power of email. And Facebook. And Twitter. And LinkedIn, Pinterest, Instagram, iTunes, YouTube and more.

But he'd rather make those always important face-to-face connections, nurturing strong, lasting bonds, and collaborating on things that matter.

So much so, **he's considered one of America's foremost authorities on the building social capital, influence, management, culture change and leadership**...

- Corporate executives rely on his expertise to help with culture change, teaching leadership and management skill sets, improving performance and profit, and simplifying organizational processes.
- Successful people come to him when they are lost and don't know where they want to go next in their career.
- Charities seek him out to promote events and raise money.
- Entrepreneurs come to him for help on managing their businesses, finding new investments, and building relationships to find new opportunities.

Mastering relationships and understanding human behavior are his calling cards.

You should listen to him if you believe relationships will play a major role in your success in business and in life. Because at his core, he believes EVERYTHING we accomplish is with or through other people.

Unfortunately, one doesn't learn Jason's breakthrough social skills in school or just by luck. We are living in an era where people have the worst communication and social skills ever.

We rely on technology far too much, creating a society that substitutes authentic relationships with transient, superficial, and virtual ones. We see this example every day with people who would rather text than talk.

As a result, our lack of social skills holds us back from truly creating the business success and fulfillment we are capable of. We build walls instead of creating stronger bonds.

This causes us to miss out on the truly amazing people that we are meant to meet, but often don't. We reach out only when we need to get a customer, create a joint venture, to get a task or project done or...to get something we want in any area of our lives. And even then, if we can avoid really connecting (and being vulnerable), that's preferable.

This strategy compromises not only our success, but our happiness, love and the passion in our lives.

The good news is you don't have to be the most popular kid in school to learn Jason's brand of social, communication, emotional and leadership strategies. You don't need charisma. You don't have to be beautiful. You don't have to be a celebrity. You don't have to be a CEO like Richard Branson. You don't have to know lot of people already. You don't have to have a lot of time.

You can start right where you are. And, yes, this covers introverts too.

Jason is fond of saying his local contact list in Dallas has grown to over 15,000+. And he started it just a few short years ago when he first moved there.

Amazing, but true.

Imagine you are maintaining a contact list of 15,000. Imagine the wonderfully close, personal friendships... the business associates... the colleagues... the opportunities... you name it... and creating a business, career, and life on your terms.

**Imagine how you could change your life
and the world around you.**

Your social, communication and emotional skills determine:

- Your ability to lead and manage others
- Your likeability
- Your ability to persuade and influence people
- Your ability to build the business or career of your dreams
- Your ability to attract customers, partners, investors, bankers, and more
- Your ability to connect with others, and create true belonging
- Your ability to make a difference in someone's life or business

And the best place to start is by reading this information-packed book. Multiple times. Then implementing as you go step-by-step.

You can start by connecting with people from your past. Reaching out to one or two new people today. It doesn't take much to get the ball rolling.

Consider these ideas business and life essentials. I strongly encourage you to put Jason's strategies into action in your own life.

I can guarantee the rewards personally, socially, emotionally, and financially will be profound and lasting.

Rick Duris
Founder and Creator of CopyRanger.com

INTRODUCTION

"There is no such thing as a 'self-made' man. We are made up of thousands of others. Everyone who has ever done a kind deed for us, or spoken one word of encouragement to us, has entered into the make-up of our character and of our thoughts, as well as our success."
—*George Burton Adams*

Do you ever...

- Feel awkward or fearful about approaching people to start conversations?
- Not know what to say when you're chatting with someone and think they will judge you if you say something wrong?
- Not know how to break into group conversations?
- Feel uncomfortable or have social anxiety when you are out among acquaintances or people you don't know?
- Struggle to build deep and meaningful relationships with others that leave you happy and truly fulfilled?
- Feel like you have little or no understanding of how to successfully build your business network?
- Not know how to advance your career or start your own business because you can't meet the right people to help you (i.e., investors, board members, venture capitalists, mentors, or executives)?
- Feel frustrated in your sales or business development efforts because you can't seem to find the right customers or partners?

- Struggle to influence others and build consensus within your company or business?
- Feel like you struggle to create a successful romantic relationship or interactions with the opposite sex?
- Feel overwhelmed and way too busy to find the time for meeting people and building relationships in any area of your life?

Don't worry. We've all been there. Building highly successful and effective relationships and collaborations with others is extremely hard to do. And it's not an innate skill we are born with; relationship building requires learned behaviors, skills, and habits. That's why you have to build a focused plan for your life for all your relationships and develop the specific behaviors, mindsets, and habits to get whatever you want in your life.

Along with that…nothing in your life is compartmentalized; everything you do affects everything else. What you do in your personal life affects what happens in your career or business, and vice versa.

We are the sum of our relationships and the people we spend the most time with. We do almost everything in life with or through other people. Relationship mastery is essential to an extraordinary business and life. We've seen in our own lives and through the stories of other people, the pain, heartache, and destruction that can happen when we don't master this area.

A critical life strategy and the new currency for creating an extraordinary life is GIVING (along with helping and inspiring others). When you let go of the mentality of "What's in it for me?" or "What can I get before others get something from me?" you discover opportunities to feel fulfilled, happy, loved, and passionate, and you have the opportunity to create the life you really want to live. It's whom you meet and what you create with them along your journey that will shape your life and the results you get. Bottom line: the sum of your relationships and the ability to master your own psychology, which includes your thought patterns, mindsets, emotions, and habits, will equal the quality of your life experiences. So if you want to create your extraordinary business and life, you have to get them both right.

With the rise of the Internet, technology, smartphones, and social media, an interesting—and alarming—shift has taken place in the last two decades. As a society, rather than becoming more capable of human connection, we have become more and more isolated from one another. Yet it's relationships that are absolutely critical and essential to driving both professional and personal success.

By substituting social media and technology for real human connections, working remotely by ourselves, participating less in group activities and organizations, and living in a "rootless" world where people move from city to city often with very few connections, we're eroding and losing touch with valuable communication, social, and human interaction skills. We are using social media and technology as a way to be noticed by others, and often seek validation through "likes," "retweets," etc. We are living in the online world more than the real world. A recent Harris Poll study found that Americans would rather give up sex than their smartphones.

Let's face it, how many of us have our smartphones within arm's length 24/7 or close to it? How many times do you see people texting continuously at a restaurant, bar, or event, when they are with friends, family, a date, or next to someone they could meet? People are not even present in their lives with people who are right in front of them!

With all of this going on, meeting new people and growing relationships on any level is getting much harder, not easier. People aren't learning social, communication, or relationship skills in the education system. Instead they have to trust the school of hard knocks, their street smarts, a mentor/coach, or a book. Today, almost everyone is struggling and overwhelmed by how to put what they learn into action—how to find and develop new friends, business colleagues, and romantic relationships, and create a meaningful life. Many people are just giving up and feel hopeless and lost, and they disengage from the world around them or self-medicate with drugs, alcohol, prescriptions, etc. In this way, they create a cycle of failure in their relationships and enter new toxic relationships...over and over again.

All of this is creating a culture where people are substituting authentic relationships with virtual ones, and it is quickly eroding our ability to communicate in the real world. While networking sites such as LinkedIn can be helpful, many people use tools like this to avoid making an effort to meet and communicate with people *in the flesh.* Firing off emails has its function in business, but picking up the phone, having a face-to-face lunch, saying hi to people down the hall, or scheduling an in-person coffee meeting is much more fulfilling and ultimately more rewarding. Plus, people don't build deep, meaningful relationships on email or the Internet in the same way that they do in person.

To create lasting connections, we have to consciously buck the trend and take a much more deliberate, intentional, and focused approach to meeting people and relationship building. Doing this means being vulnerable, authentic, and transparent, and we must prioritize people and giving without having to get something in return. Being connected with other people increases happiness and love, creates unlimited opportunities, and motivates us to create the life we really want. To become the best we can be, we need to enlist others to help us. And we need to help others get what they want in order for us to get what we want. We also need to introduce new people into our personal, social, and business lives on a regular basis. Every person can impact your life in a different way no matter who they are, where they are from, or what they do. By not doing this, we miss out on the chance to learn and absorb ideas and inspiration from unexpected sources.

Right now, something is less than perfect in your personal and business life. You are looking to quickly and artfully build, manage, and grow new and existing relationships in your life. That's why you're reading this book.

Maybe your dating life isn't what you want it to be. When you go out, maybe you stare across the room, hoping to meet someone, but at the end of the night, you inevitably go home alone, feeling disappointed and depressed. Or you have an existing relationship or marriage that has hit a low or rocky point, and you want to take it to extraordinary levels.

Maybe your networking skills aren't where you'd like them to be and you are stuck. You know what you want from your network—top-level career choices, opportunities to build your own business, and financial freedom—but you have no idea how to build, cultivate, manage, and tap into it.

Maybe you are struggling in business because you can't get proper mentorship in your company, you can't take your sales career to the next level, you are unable to influence the board of directors or executive leadership, or build consensus with your executive team to move ideas forward.

Maybe your friendships are in need of a jumpstart. Rather than putting energy into friendships that don't make you feel good, you want to start spending time with amazing people who are successful, active, positive, and fun, who challenge you and push you forward. Or perhaps tap into the social opportunities where you access amazing people and artists, enjoy exclusive access to events or parties, tap into leading thinkers or creative minds, enjoy amazing hidden beauty in the world, and much more.

Maybe you're just tired of spending so much time alone, isolated, disconnected, frustrated, rudderless, unhappy, unfulfilled, and sleepwalking through your life.

If any of the above sounds like you, you're in the right place. I'm going to help you master meeting people in a new way that will bring more people than you ever thought possible into your life. I will help you build deeper, more meaningful, and amazing relationships that unleash true joy, love, and happiness. The social life you're going to develop is going to build your social capital in a way that will open the doors to limitless possibilities in every area of your life. You can do this on your terms, not anyone else's. This means you won't need to try to convince people to like you; they will like you for who you are (and for who you are becoming). I won't let you fail.

How do I know this will work for you? Over the past decade, I've built a network of more than 15,000 people in Dallas alone, and that number continues to grow locally and globally. I'm meeting and interacting with hundreds of people every single week, and involved with dozens of organizations, along with planning small- and large-scale charity and nonprofit events in my free time. I've spoken to hundreds of leading experts on mastering psychology and overcoming obstacles and your past, creating influence and behavior change, developing social and communication skills, meeting and networking with people, building extraordinary relationships, creating your dream job, building friendships, and much more.

I've taught thousands of people to successfully do everything I'm going teach you. In fact, many people have met hundreds of new people in our very first month of working together, and some of those have turned into best friends, business partners, marathon buddies, relationships and marriages, and have led to extraordinary opportunities in their lives.

I've been in the trenches for more than a decade learning why people do the things they do in their personal and business lives, along with the motivations and the psychology behind their choices. I've learned to help people master their own psychology, along with crucial people and relationship skills, to get what they want.

This process will be simple, fun, and innovative, and although I'll teach you shortcuts and ways to create success significantly faster, you must buy into the entire process. Buy-in is necessary to learn anything in life because you must listen, be engaged and believe the information, and then act with certainty and focus to get the results you want. You will have to push past the resistance that comes up as well as the old programming—the way you have been doing things.

Sometimes you may have to go with the flow, enjoy the experience, and try out the information. Remember, you can always go back to your old beliefs and the life you had been living. Treat it like an experiment and do something new. You have nothing to lose and everything to gain.

I know some people may be thinking, "Well, I'm not sure I can do this!" Trust me, you can. It doesn't matter if your current social and communication skills are less than great or if you suffer from social anxiety and fears that are holding you back. Your educational or economic background, appearance, and intelligence doesn't matter—you can do this.

If your life is in a rut, I will show you quick and easy ways to meet new people and help you create an authentic rapport with those around you very quickly, as you'll also learn how to develop new and existing amazing relationships. I will also teach you how to create social capital—the key to your long-term success—by leveraging network groups and creating your personal brand. By adopting a few easy behavioral changes, you're going to be dramatically more effective in relationships and collaborations in your personal and business lives than you ever thought you could be.

To get something you've never had before, you must do something you've never done. Those new experiences open our eyes and minds to what we can change, and the limitless and extraordinary opportunities that lie ahead in life.

I'm going to provide you with the playbook to create a life of social freedom. And I'll show you how to do it in the shortest amount of time with the maximum impact. In the process, you're going to have a lot of fun, and by the end you'll have more confidence than you've ever had before.

One last thing I want to mention is a frustrating part of learning to master meeting people and building relationships.

There are books and information on business relationships and personal relationships, but really nothing that tackles *all* your interactions and relationships.

Instead, once you learn the information, it's up to you to integrate it in different contexts. That gets really complicated and it can be overwhelming. Well, a significant amount of information can be applied to *every* area of your life, and every person you interact with could potentially be integrated in many different areas in your life. Of course, there are specific strategies and tools for business networking as opposed to dating and relationships. And I'll be sharing those distinctions, as well as the commonalities, as we move forward together.

I want to start by giving you a peek into what you will be learning and the skills you will be developing. There are eight key components to supercharging your relationships.

<u>Supercharger #1: Putting People First:</u> Imagine that every weekend, you're invited to so many events, you couldn't attend them all even if you wanted to. Emails and phone calls arrive offering high-paying jobs, introductions to new professional networks, and terrific investment opportunities. You have unlimited opportunities with the opposite sex and feel fully in control of your dating life. If you are in a relationship or marriage, both you and your partner feel fulfilled, happy, and like you are on a successful road together. Most importantly, others become more successful because of your help. People are inspired to be around you because you put others first. You've built a highly successful network of people in every area of your life. You can have it all, and you don't have to settle. Sure, you may have to make some tradeoffs, but that's much different than lowering your standards for what you want your life to be. In order to do this, you have to prioritize meeting people and building relationships as number one on your list. Without prioritizing this, you will encounter a lot of challenges, heartache, disappointments, and failed interactions and relationships.

Supercharger #2: Seeing Every Opportunity: Everywhere you go is a potential meeting place. I've met fantastic people in line at Starbucks, at the grocery store, and waiting in line at the dry cleaners. Some of my best friends now laugh about how we met somewhere just like this. What became a great relationship started with a simple, quick conversation. Every relationship starts with an initial interaction. Think of it as five-minute conversations that turn into lifelong relationships. The more people you meet, the more opportunities you have to create abundance and learn life skills, and you'll also have a greater chance of meeting the right people for yourself and others. I'll show you the ultimate power of networking in groups, building your social capital, and how to manage it all.

Supercharger #3: Realizing, Not Rationalizing: Stop rationalizing why you are not meeting other people or building the relationships you want. Stop using the excuses that you don't have time, you don't know what to do, you can't do that and/or you're *just not good at it.* Those days are over for you! You are truly limitless now.

Supercharger #4: Starting Simply, Simply Starting: All it takes is a few words, "How's everything?" or "How's your week going?" to meet new people. That's it. Just take the first step and start with a simple, short communication. It's not complex, but a lot of people overthink this, giving themselves an excuse not to put themselves out there. Because your energy and vibe is much more important than what you say! Delivery trumps content. I'll show you how to start any conversation and never run out of things to say.

Supercharger #5: Conquering Fear: We're constantly comparing our life to what we see on our friends' Facebook newsfeeds. It's easy to think that everyone else has a great life, while you're still struggling in yours. Well, realize that most people don't share their skeletons on Facebook. No one's life is perfect, and everyone struggles with fear of failure and fear of rejection. You are not alone. *Realize that you have the power to move forward and create what you want.* Though you may never completely eliminate all your fears, they can be managed and you can understand them much better. Lead with authenticity, vulnerability, transparency, giving, and having fun.

Supercharger #6: Empowering Yourself: Your success is directly correlated to your psychology because your thoughts turn into the actions you take and the results you generate. Your mind is extremely powerful, and it will either propel you forward or cripple you. You need clarity, focus, and compelling motivations to move toward the life you want. It's critical to remove inner conflicts that may be holding you back as well. You also need to create your life plan, and understand why you want what you want in your life. Don't live your life as a sailboat hoping to drift to the right destination without a map or GPS; your chance of getting where you want to go is very low.

Supercharger #7: Loving Learning: *Social skills are learned behaviors, not something you are born with.* Anyone can learn to master being social, no matter what your background is, what you look like, or where you went to school. It just takes practice. If you commit daily to this process, you are bound to have success. It is a lot like working out. You get very sore initially as you break down the muscle, but you are building it back much stronger. Well, when you first go out to meet people it is a process and it takes time to improve, and it won't go well all the time. You are going to have rough days. But you will learn from this, get back up, implement a new way of doing something, move forward, and create breakthroughs. This is a very healthy process in life, and you have to learn to laugh at yourself and embrace your path.

Supercharger #8: Emotions, Like Intellect, Must be Mastered: You are going to have to master your emotions on your life journey if you want to be successful. One question that comes up a lot from clients is, "How do I stop being jealous? Or angry? Or nervous? Or envious?" Well, first you change your psychology and how you interpret and process information in your brain. That will help you see the world differently and eliminate the thought from occurring. But some negative emotions will seep through no matter what you do. You can't control every emotion you feel, BUT you can control how you behave and act (or react to it). For example: "I am angry," is a lot different than "I feel angry." You may feel anger when something happens, but you don't need to act or dwell on it. Language is very powerful, so notice how you use it and how subtle changes can make huge differences.

The next question that comes up from clients is, "How do you deal with worry, failure, rejection, and loss?" I acknowledge and accept the emotion, and act positively, moving forward in my life instead of getting bogged down in the negativity. I've created a habit around doing it. For example, some days I don't want to exercise in the morning and I'd rather sleep. I feel the emotion that I am sleepy and this sucks that I have to drag myself out of bed. I accept those emotions and feelings, take responsibility for them, and then go straight to my workout class. I don't let the thoughts control me or stop me from doing what I need to do for myself. If you try to stop the negative thought, you will focus on it. And what you focus on grows stronger over time and will suck you in like a black hole.

So here's what you do: Feel the emotion, acknowledge it, take responsibility for it, and act in spite of it. Not "I am not angry at my boss," but "I am feeling anger towards my boss." You have control over it. You can accept and move past it to do your job and work effectively with your boss and colleagues. Alternatively, you can use gratitude to help here. You can say, "I am grateful for feeling nervous when I make this new sales presentation to a client." You accept the emotion and diffuse it with gratitude so you can move past it quickly to take the action of presenting to the new client. That's a process that will help you move past mental blocks if your negative thoughts consistently control you. This will also help move past procrastination or lack of motivation as well.

In this book, you're going to learn how to:

- Master your mindset and emotions to create the confidence, certainty, and positivity to meet people and build deeper, more trusting relationships.
- Create your life plan to foster clarity, focus, and certainty about where you are headed, along with how to brand yourself.
- Use giving to set yourself apart and fuel relationship building.
- Open up and let others in by being vulnerable, transparent, authentic, and honest.
- Identify good places to meet people, what to do, what to say, and how to follow up to create a life where people love to be around you.
- Overcome career- and business-crippling habits and inner conflicts.
- Manage, filter, and prioritize your relationship networks in your personal and business life and build closer relationships than you ever thought possible.
- Create a "people plan" to meet the individuals you need to advance your career or business and develop mutual success.
- Build social capital to create a powerful personal brand to develop a magnetic reputation, wield significant influence, and achieve massive success.
- Leverage the secrets of networking and group dynamics to unleash social influence and power, while helping and inspiring others.
- Recruit and engage others to cheer you on and help you

reach your dreams, while eliminating the "score card" or transaction mentality in your relationships.

- Cultivate successful relationships with VIPs and influencers.
- Achieve unlimited success by leveraging the power of your network to find opportunities, share information, and tap into massive resources.
- Leverage your social media presence to expand your online presence, increase your reputation, and manage your relationships.
- Make the most of personal assets such as style.

Ready? **Let's get started!**

CHAPTER 1

SOCIAL CAPITAL: HOW TO RULE THE SOCIAL UNIVERSE

"Your time is limited, so don't waste it living someone else's life. Don't be trapped by dogma—which is living with the results of other people's thinking. Don't let the noise of others' opinions drown out your own inner voice. And most important, have the courage to follow your heart and intuition. They somehow already know what you truly want to become. Everything else is secondary."

—*Steve Jobs*

What kind of currency is more valued than a hundred-dollar bill, more compact than a quarter, and accepted in every country? It's social capital, and it's part of what's going to help you meet people and build incredible relationships. Social capital is critical to your success, building your extraordinary life, and ruling the social universe. Why? The greater your social capital, the more opportunities, access, and resources you will have to get what you want in life, the more relationships you will have, and the faster your relationships will progress.

There are two ways to dramatically and exponentially increase your social capital and distinguish yourself from others. First, it is through truly giving to others because you care about them, while at the same time not expecting anything in return. You are giving with no strings attached. Secondly, you can build trust and reciprocity much faster through meeting people in social and business groups and organizations. This allows you to meet more people and build relationships exponentially faster than in other environments.

Ultimately, you'll master the art and science of social capitalism by integrating the key disciplines outlined below.

Social capital is generated when you invest in your relationships and networks and add value to them. Your social capital grows when others see or perceive you as someone who's known, admired, and trusted. Accumulating social capital increases your influence, power, reach, trustworthiness, reciprocity, and social status. The other big advantage of social capital is that others will want you to succeed and will do whatever they can to help you or provide you with needed resources and knowledge.

What is Social Capital?

A concept that has been around since the early 1900s, social capital is broadly defined as the resources that individuals access and generate through their business and personal networks. These resources reside in networks of relationships, rather than in any one individual. These resources consist of information, ideas, power, influence, reciprocity, giving or generosity, financial capital, business opportunities, status, trust, cooperation, and other factors.

According to one of the earliest leading thinkers on social capital, Robert Putnam: "Whereas physical capital refers to physical objects and human capital refers to the properties of individuals, social capital refers to connections among individuals—social networks and the norms of reciprocity and trustworthiness that arise from them. In that sense social capital is closely related to what some have called 'civic virtue.' The difference is that 'social capital' calls attention to the fact that civic virtue is most powerful when embedded in a sense network of reciprocal social relations. A society of many virtuous but isolated individuals is not necessarily rich in social capital."

Social capital also creates personal or economic benefits derived from creating strong social networks that include shared values, resources and information, and a sense of belonging. We build social capital by creating new ties and strengthening old ones. These connections will increase an individual's quality of life and opportunities by linking people more closely to their town or city and to larger societal resources. This process builds connections by strengthening bonds that link people, and it bridges differences or distinctions between them.

Individual social capital depends on a contact network that reaches across various social and professional groups. To generate social capital, this network must be skillfully and intentionally constructed and maintained. Trust is the glue that holds individuals, groups, and networks together, and it is the essential ingredient for successfully building social capital. Trust eliminates the need to negotiate with each person for business or personal collaborations, sharing, or intimacy. It is similar to why creating an agreed-upon currency system such as cash is more efficient than bartering in every transaction.

Why is this? The main factors are predictability and reliability in other people's behavior, motivations, and actions. Trust also entails evidence or a feeling that someone is moral, generous, honest, and competent, along with having integrity. For example, "I trust he will follow through with his or her offer to help me do XYZ." The key here is that people do some sort of risk assessment or calculation in their minds that is analytical and/or emotional before giving trust. Many times this is done in seconds or minutes. So leading by giving versus taking is an extremely powerful trust-building action.

Trust is very powerful because it enables greater levels of reciprocity (i.e., giving and receiving) between people to collaborate, share resources, and interact on an intimate level, which expands opportunities for everyone involved. Reciprocity typically involves economic or emotional exchanges. Reciprocity also typically involves giving to others without the expectation of something in return for a particular interaction or transaction.

Ultimately, trust shifts to loyalty (which can include love and/or a deep sense of connection along with admiration and respect) that opens up limitless possibilities in our business and personal lives. That's when you maximize your currency in social capital. Finally, you will have a continuum of people in your life, from people who have a deep love for you (i.e., best friends, business or marriage partners, etc.) to people who share common beliefs and attitudes (i.e., acquaintances or strangers you only meet once).

The key here is to be able to move people from the initial encounter through the trust stage into the loyalty stage quickly, and keep them there. Think of it as planting the seeds of social capital and growing them over time with repeated interactions and delving into more personal conversations that transition from "yours and mine" to a collective "ours." A critical skill that a social capitalist learns is how to accumulate, maintain, and grow the number of deep and meaningful relationships, and how to let go of those relationships that no longer serve them.

This is how people become "super networkers" who have tens of thousands of contacts and a vast number of intimate relationships. It is a major misconception that you can't have a large number of close, loyal, loving, and deep connections with people. It's very possible if you manage and care for your networks. And even if you only want a few great relationships, creating and harnessing your social capital will help you find the right extraordinary people for you.

The challenge here is that studies point out we are at an all-time low in trusting others, and it's the major hurdle in meeting other people.

So how do you build trust? Trust is built more easily and more quickly under the following conditions:

1) Repeated exposure to the same people on a consistent basis, which tends to lead to greater confidence that

others can be trusted, especially inside of social or business groups or organizations.

2) When an individual knows you have someone in common, a sort of social obligation forms because of the common bond, so both of you will typically extend yourselves more for each other than you would for a complete stranger.

3) Typically, the physical proximity of people to each other matters, but in a mobile world it's not a limiting factor.

4) People are honest, transparent, direct, and adept in their social and communication skills. Their words and actions match up and you see their character shine through.

5) People lead with giving and generosity without being attached to what they get back, versus purely taking or transacting. You also truly care about the other person and what happens to them.

6) People follow through with the actions they've promised in a timely fashion, and you can count on them when you need them.

Don't forget, your personal and professional reputation can add or subtract from your ability to build trust with others. So how people collectively view you and the number of "raving" fans you have will influence the process here.

Access to your social capital depends on the size, scope, and quality of your personal and business networks, along with the ability to reach those people you don't know in your indirect networks. This access allows you to achieve personal and business goals, fulfill your purpose in life, develop deep and meaningful relationships, and create an extraordinary life without limits. Many people falsely believe they fail or succeed based on their own efforts. The fact is, we need others. The fairy tale of individualism is dead. If you think you can go it alone, you're bound to be disappointed and you will eventually hit a dead end in your life.

Social Capital and Your Personal Brand

Your personal brand (i.e., your image, identity, and perceived value) plays a large role in building and defining your social capital, which helps you attract and engage people and develop your relationships. In chapter four, we'll discuss creating your life plan, and that's the first step in really figuring out your brand and what you stand for.

Your brand is about who you are as a person, how you are perceived, and what you stand for. It's what you uniquely stand for, and a strategy and roadmap for how to act. Others will tell you what your brand is based on their experiences with you, the things that they see you doing, and what they hear about you from others. The way they see you behaving most consistently and frequently is how they will see and perceive your personal brand. Everyone has one, whether they know it or not. So take control of it, define it, and live it on your terms. This dovetails with our conversation on trust. Your brand is the primary way you will establish your credibility with others in every area of your life—business, personal, etc. So purposely create it.

Your personal brand will help you navigate difficult situations, make better decisions in life, communicate better with others, and be an admired leader. For example, in work and in your career, it will help you take more ownership in projects and outcomes, and communicate better with others so they see you are passionately invested in everyone's success. The flip side is many people just go through the motions during work without thinking about how they present themselves to others. Your personal brand gets you engaged with yourself and others, and helps you identify how to create winning outcomes that benefit people and your organization.

Here are a few pointers on how to start identifying your personal brand:

Step 1: Get feedback from others so you can see where you are today. There is a great free 360-degree survey by Adam Grant at giveandtake.com/Home/RequestAssessment that you can send to friends, colleagues, etc. I'd send this to 5–10 people in different areas of your life so you can get a full spectrum of analysis. You can also develop your own personal short survey with surveymonkey.com or other tools.

Step 2: Brainstorm what you want to be known for. Write out your strengths when it comes to skills and abilities, experience, personality traits, etc. What are you best at? What are you most proud of? Think of a time when you were at your best. Think of a time when you were proud of yourself.

Step 3: Compare your list to the comments from people in Step 1. What stands out? What is distinctive in your mind?

Step 4: On a piece of paper or online, make two columns. In the first column, describe in two or three words how you want to be known. For example, "strategic, calm communicator." Or, "fearless, giving leader." Or, "rising above obstacles." This is your brand.

Step 5: In the second column: What five behaviors and actions would someone with this brand exhibit? For example, if your brand is "rising above obstacles," you will want to introduce solutions to major challenges faced by your clientele. If your brand is "fearless, giving leader," you are going to want to empower and support others to take risks, and help them get needed resources and information. This will help you see how to apply this information in your personal, business, and social lives.

When you have completed this exercise, you can use this as a guide in your everyday life. I'd also incorporate this into your style of dress and the clothes you choose. You want to make sure your external self is congruent with your personal brand. Finally, think about how you communicate on social media channels and ponder creating your own website where you can discuss issues or areas that you are passionate about. You can take it further by doing public speaking in a particular area, writing and contributing articles to your favorite publications, pitching ideas to bloggers or media, starting a podcast, teaching a class or workshop at your company, etc. As an experienced marketer, I can tell you that doing these things will really separate you from others and take your brand to the next level.

The Life Cycle of Social Capital

I want to show you how social capital can play out in your life to show you its power. Then we will dissect what makes it all possible and why. Ok, let's say you go to an event one evening that you've never gone to before. This might be an event related to a charity, nonprofit, business, or perhaps a personal interest. You chat with people during a reception, and within an hour, you've met 20 people. You introduce people to each other and help other people meet new friends, business contacts, and more. You exchange contact information with 10 people.

The next day you add them on your social networks, follow up with everyone, and invite them to another activity or event you are doing that week on Thursday, along with a brunch you are planning that Saturday. Midweek, you get invited to a great, free outdoor concert that you then invite your contacts to on Facebook. Also, during one of your conversations, you find out that one person is looking for a job in sales, so you connect her with the vice president of sales in your company. Finally, another person mentions he wants to run a marathon and you connect him to a friend of yours who has run several of them.

Two successful business executives indicate that they want to join you on Thursday, and two people who are on high profile boards are open for brunch on Saturday. You then call and make reservations at a great new brunch spot that you find on CultureMap, UrbanDaddy, Yelp!, or Google. You get a table for six even though only two respond because you will run across more people who may want to join you. You also research venues close to your Thursday event so everyone can continue to have fun after the event. And so on and so forth.

That's the path to social capital. It's not that hard, and you aren't spending money to do it. Also, think about this: If you did this two times a week, you could meet a couple hundred new people a month and more than 2,000 people a year. Do you see how you can be the social hub bringing people together? You are introducing them to each other at the event you are going to, setting up brunch, adding value to their specific needs, etc. You are helping them by expanding their social circles to create opportunities in every area of their lives. *You* are the force or glue that brings and binds those people together. When they say how they met, it's through you. When I've done this, I've helped people find best friends, business partners, job opportunities, activity partners, get funding for their startups, investment opportunities and marriages.

There is a huge opportunity to meet people in social or business organizations and groups. They typically are more active, involved, and go out more. If you make a habit of going out in your city or town, you'll see a lot of the same people over and over again that you met at an event, function, etc. They'll introduce you to their friends and greet you like a friend because of the trust you've earned as a part of their social group. This allows you to access their "indirect network," (i.e., people in other people's networks) providing you with additional ways to meet people quickly, and much more easily than you would by approaching strangers.

Via your new and developing connections, you will get invited to more private events and functions. These will be other opportunities to meet people. An average person will get invited to two to five private events per month if they invest in their social capital. People will also proactively invite you to public events such as charity happy hours and galas, restaurant and bar openings, festivals, and more. Through this process, you will begin to meet VIPs, successful business people, and high-status people in your city who will give you even greater access to other opportunities. There are unlimited business opportunities that go along with this.

Once you've established your social network, you can choose to throw your own parties and meet many more people. Others recognize your social capital. They will instantly extend you more trust and status than they would to strangers because of who you are and how you act. Before you know it, your social networks (online and offline) will extend well beyond your own city, state, or country.

How to Maximize Social Capital

Your social capital is directly proportional to the size, diversity, and quality of your personal and business networks. Meeting people in groups or organizations is the fastest and most efficient way to accumulate and manage your social capital, and is the least resource intensive. You are leveraging "the network effect" and group dynamics to build your social capital. You also tap into the ability to accelerate trust and reciprocity. This is the secret that super networkers use to consistently meet a lot of new people. It's why the networks of the rich get richer.

Here are some points to keep in mind about social capital:

- As the degree of social connections (i.e., friends in common, shared networks, belonging to the same groups, general commonalities, etc.) and shared interests between people increases, so does their trust with each other.
- There is generally some level of immediate trust associated within groups that enables more openness and acceptance of new individuals to the group.
- Typically, there is reciprocity between individuals in

groups, including new members, which speeds up the relationship-building process, allowing people to help others more freely and share resources.

- As trust builds, people can access the business and personal networks of the other individuals in their groups to increase their own networks.

- Your ability to be open, direct, vulnerable, authentic, honest, and giving in large and small group settings, as well as in one-on-one settings, impacts the rate at which you move interactions into relationships.

- If people lead with generosity in their interactions, they can build massive social capital regardless of their education, background, appearance, or other factors.

- Your ability to meet new people increases over time because people behave in a more trustworthy manner toward people with social capital.

- People exert more influence if they are admired by others. Admiration stems from people's perception of an individual having high (or moral) character. People see an individual's words lining up with their actions in a true sense of caring about others, versus solely advancing their own needs.

- Research has shown that individuals who spend time volunteering, and those with more close friends and bigger networks, are much better at eliciting trust from other people.

- Aligning yourself with people who have powerful, large networks and who are recognized influencers can have a major impact on your network. We will discuss later how to meet VIPs and how to network with them. Again here, trust is a major part of the connection. They need to know you don't have ulterior motives to get something, you are trying to connect with them as people and not "stars," and that you aren't into gossiping (don't be TMZ!).

Ultimately, people with strong social capital become hubs linking groups and individuals and groups to other groups, and through that function, they can exert a significant amount of influence and power in society—locally and globally—and can uncover unlimited opportunities in any of area of life.

Out with the Old, In with the New

Meeting people one by one, though traditional for dating, friendships, and business, is a thing of the past. Today, it's a recipe that leads to scarcity, disappointment, and disillusionment. It also leads to poor social and communication skills.

Here is how it typically works:

- When you are out at bars, restaurants, grocery store, and coffees shops, you meet people randomly. You rarely if ever access charity, nonprofit, business, or networking events. You get invited to a party or two here and there, but pretty infrequently.
- In addition, in these environments, you're approaching people "cold" (i.e., without an introduction from someone else), when their defense mechanisms are up. This lowers your success rate.
- When you run into someone you know, they will introduce you to whomever they are with, but this happens infrequently since you have a small social circle, and your success varies on your trust and status.
- To help with this, you may join an interest group or two, but you don't maximize its potential opportunities.
- In the end, you have a handful of friends and work colleagues, and rarely meet new people and develop new friendships and/or relationships. You know the importance of networking for jobs, but you never really do it. You miss out on business opportunities (board seats, investments, great jobs, new clients, etc.)

all the time because you don't have access to the right people at the right time. You feel disconnected, not a part of the world around you, and you lack the deep relationships you truly want, but you're not sure what to do about it.

You get the idea here. I bet you can relate to the scenario above. So what's the new normal? Growing and maximizing your social capital by meeting people through groups, organizations, and events.

What Social Capital Can Do for You

Social capital is more than just your network, connections, and relationships. Your ability to create your extraordinary life is directly tied to and significantly enhanced with the skills you learn building your social capital. For example:

- Social, communication, and interpersonal skills are critical for any interactions and relationships. They are learned behaviors and require practice.
- If you only know five people, then your choice of a best friend is pretty limited. Many people settle in their personal life because of this scarcity, but what if your network expanded to thousands of people?
- Social capital creates more experiences with people, which in turn helps you learn more about yourself, understand other people better, and recognize how to build deep, successful, and truly meaningful relationships in your personal and business life.
- Social capital provides "life insurance" for free to you. People will proactively look out for you and steer you away from problematic situations or people. You will avoid a lot of problems and negativity you might otherwise encounter.
- Foundational to the process is giving, helping, and

inspiring. This truly deepens relationships on the highest level.

- Social capital builds extraordinary habits and life skills to move your life forward and help you avoid pitfalls such as comparison, seeking external validation or approval, worrying about what other people think all the time, etc.
- Social capital has long been recognized as a key factor in becoming a standout in any professional setting. In a study done at Bell Labs twenty years ago, relationship networks were identified as a key differentiator for the high performers.
- Social capital has been tied to increased levels of happiness in several studies.

Easy Ways to Build Social Capital

Building social capital is simple. You don't have to wait for the perfect moment to begin. You can get started building social capital today. Here are a few ideas:

1. Volunteer.
2. Organize a brunch with new and old friends.
3. Call someone from your past to catch up.
4. Learn a new hobby or interest.
5. Join a running group or athletic team.
6. Donate to a local organization.
7. Say hello to everyone you meet.
8. Get to know restaurant managers, bartenders, and other service people.
9. Each week, send an email to three people you know thanking them for something they've done for you.
10. Forgive someone from your past. You don't need to contact them. Forgiveness is more about you than them.
11. Hold open the door for someone.
12. Invite a stranger to join you at an activity of an event.

13. Start a new tradition.
14. Listen to someone instead of talk.
15. Make someone laugh.
16. Plan a charity event or charity happy hour.

Many of the ideas above take only take seconds or minutes to do. You will have many opportunities each day to do *something*. And this is a very small list—the possibilities are endless.

I hope that you are starting to understand the importance of social capital in your life and how to cultivate it. You can find additional resources on my website, JasonTreu.com.

Next, I want to share with you my story. As you'll see, I wasn't born with amazing social and communication skills— far from it!

CHAPTER 2

MY STORY: BLOOD, SWEAT, TEARS, & ACTION

"Daring greatly means the courage to be vulnerable. It means to show up and be seen. To ask for what you need. To talk about how you are feeling. To have the hard conversations."

—*Brene Brown*

I may be an extrovert, that doesn't mean that meeting people always came naturally to me. Back in college, I was the typical social overachiever and involved in every activity and organization you can imagine. I was even the Student Body Treasurer at Indiana University in Bloomington and on the homecoming court. I had amazing opportunities and a lot of fantastic friends, and pretty much complete social freedom. I could walk into a bar by myself and spend hours catching up with people I already knew. When my parents came to visit me, they would often get annoyed because we couldn't make it down the street without me talking to several people and making us late for the next thing we were supposed to do.

I went on to get my law degree and masters degree in Communications in New York, moved to Los Angeles briefly, and then to San Francisco, where I spent seven years. I met a lot of people in San Francisco, but I never seemed to have the social success that I'd had back in school. I couldn't really complain because I always had fun things to do, great friends, job opportunities and abundance in my life. But my social life felt like a lot of work. I also felt like something was missing or just beyond my reach, and I was trying so that people would like me. I may have seemed very confident on the outside, but fear and self-doubt were my constant companions. I got very good at concealing this from the outside world, but in fact, I couldn't let people get close to me.

When the Great Recession hit, many of my friends were laid off. It seemed like I was having a going-away party every week for someone I knew. These friends and colleagues had to move away not by choice, but by necessity. Their experience plunged me into a sea of negativity. I feared that what had happened to them could happen to me any day. On top of that, I had a couple of friends whose parents died—while still quite young—over the span of a couple months. I started to look inward, and I knew I needed to make some changes. I decided to find a way to get to Dallas, where my mother lived, so I could spend time with her while she was in the prime of her life. So many friends of my friends were moving anyway that the prospect of moving myself didn't seem so daunting.

I worked very hard networking and applying for jobs, and eventually found a position in marketing at a startup company in Dallas. It was a lucky break, but when I moved, my passion for change hit a standstill. I didn't follow through on all the things I said I was going to do and fell right back into a rut. I took one step forward and two steps backward!

A few years passed, and one night, feeling depressed, I decided to drive to the SMU campus and walk around to clear my head. It was around 10pm, so probably not the smartest thing to do, but at that time I just didn't care. I was walking through campus listening to music, when I had a major breakthrough. Why couldn't I bring my college social life back? If I'd done it then, there had to be a way to do it now. I had no clue how to begin, but I was determined. So I went back to my car and found a pen and started to brainstorm. I wrote anything that popped into my head. Later, I read it over and boy did I have a lot of BAD ideas. BUT something kept occurring to me as I read what I wrote. It was the power of meeting people in groups. I met so many people in college, not out and about, but in the organizations I belonged to. Then when I was out, I'd run into those same people and meet all of their friends. So meeting just one person in an organization could lead to meeting three or four other people. I also realized I was good at connecting people to others, and that I felt more alive when I was giving and helping others.

I started to understand the key characteristics of meeting people and why meeting people in organizations or groups was so powerful:

- The situation breaks the ice for people and naturally gives them reasons to talk to each other (i.e., What brought you here today? Are you a member organization?). People's defense mechanisms come down, more so than in clubs, bars, high-end restaurants, coffee shops...really anywhere. This makes it much easier to approach someone and start a conversation.
- It's easier to work the room and practice your social skills. Most people go out and talk to only a couple of people. They never really get warmed up or get enough practice to move them forward. In this environment, it's easy to meet more than 20 people an hour.
- It allows you to reliably see the same people several times, so you have a chance to get comfortable with them and gradually get to know them. There are always additional events or gatherings, and you can get involved as well.
- It allows you to meet people who are similar to you in terms of your hobbies, interests, and values.
- With charities, you are able to give back and help others as you meet people and have fun. You are able to meet people that value that as well. It's the one environment in which givers many times outnumber takers.

- It's somewhere where there's a core of regulars, but there are also new people to meet who are continually entering the mix. So there is always an opportunity to meet new and different people.

I went home and started looking for any groups I could think of that I might enjoy. I got on their mailing lists, joined their Facebook groups or pages, and even joined a few groups without ever going to a function. I put everything in my calendar and I was off! Kind of...

When I went to my first event, I was so nervous my mind was going a thousand miles a minute. I got myself too pumped up and became very anxious. I almost decided to drive home and skip it. But I knew if I didn't push myself forward, I would just keep making excuses, live in scarcity, and let my fears and doubts run my life. The event went well and I met a few people, but the critic in me was telling myself I had messed up. I realized, walking my dogs the next morning, that if I couldn't get my thoughts handled, I would never be able to make this journey successful.

I read many books and did a lot of self-evaluation along the way. In the process, I figured out a great way to master my thoughts, and made these key realizations:

- The story that you tell yourself about who you are is the only reality that matters, and your story manifests itself in the actions you take and results you get—your thoughts create your life.
- If you are not excited about your life and don't feel like you are making progress, you will manage to sabotage yourself every chance you get.
- If you are not clear, focused, and certain about what you want in life, you will float through life like a leaf blowing aimlessly in the wind.
- You must develop and have self-acceptance, and lose as many of your insecurities as you can. You can't

expect others to like and love you if you don't love yourself. I realize there can be a paradox here with self-improvement. The act of trying to improve yourself to many people means they are not complete or enough as they currently are. Here's how I look at it: "I am amazing, and I am enjoying and loving my journey in life of becoming more amazing." Wherever I am on my journey, I am enjoying and loving it because NOW (the present moment) is the most fantastic time in my life. So remember you are fantastic now, and in every moment going forward. Let go of that self-judgment, needless insecurity, comparing yourself to others, and telling yourself you will never win. People will admire you having this outlook and energy because it tells them you are free, strong, courageous, and positive.

Next, I read books by experts and listened to their lectures to find better ways to meet and connect with people. It turned out to be harder than I anticipated. I also spoke to business networking experts. One person whose advice really resonated with me was Keith Ferrazzi, a business relationship expert, the founder and CEO of Ferrazzi Greenlight, and a best-selling author. He really seemed to be the only person who truly got it. Although when I heard him speak, he was more focused on business networking, I could see the bridges to my social life and how to leverage the information. I came across other people, and some of the information helped, but only so much. Without experts to model success after, especially in my personal and social life, I would have to create my own success manual for mastering meeting people and building relationships.

In the process, I discovered my calling in life is to help others create their own success stories. I realized that life coaching was where I was meant to be. So I wrote a book on it, *Jump Start Your Social Life*, conducted research to see what was working and not working for people, spoke to thousands of people about their life experiences, started coaching people around the world, and created a podcast series to help people create extraordinary lives. I've always believed speaking to people who have already achieved high levels of success is a powerful way to learn.

I rolled up my sleeves and got to work. I made a plan and found a way to contact people, well-known people like the financial editor of the Today Show, Jean Chatzky; *New York Times* best-selling author and the youngest tenured professor at Wharton Adam Grant; Dr. Edna Foa, who revolutionized PTSD treatment; the CEO of Origins Recovery Center, Ben Levenson; and many others. I spoke to experts in a multitude of disciplines (art, design, finance, sports, wine, travel, business, and psychology). Through this process, I came to understand how to create extraordinary success in life, how to master my mind, build relationships, and avoid common pitfalls. It wasn't easy, but I discovered I could do anything if I set my mind to it and took action.

By the time my plan for a social life was operational, I was very involved in quite a few charity and nonprofit organizations, and I had thrown a handful of charity events with organizations and by myself. I decided I really needed to take this to the next level and see how far I could take throwing events. I sketched out some crazy ideas—one was to get the nicest penthouse in Dallas and throw a fantastic party that was for fun and not for charity. So I decided, why not! But how would I pay for it? I figured out it would cost me $20,000 or so. That's a lot of money. By enrolling other people in my purpose, I was able to fund the party. It wasn't easy, but I made it happen. It took a lot of blood, sweat, and tears to get everything together, but it ended up being a historic event with around 400 people and really showed me that anything was possible if I wanted it to be. I took what I learned from this experience and leveraged it in the more than 100 events since then I have participated in for charities and nonprofits, and I've helped raise millions of dollars. I've also sent more than a million invites for charity and nonprofit events to show people that you can help others and give, and at the same time have fun.

I feel fortunate to have the most incredible people in my life at this very moment. You, too, can be blessed with amazing people in your life if you have the courage, tenacity, love, and commitment to *take consistent actions.*

In thinking back on my journey, I want to share what my father told me the night before he died: "Son, don't waste your life and talents. I did and I regret it. Follow your dreams and make it happen. Because in the end if you don't, you will be sitting all alone wishing you would have taken the time."

I've asked a lot of older people for life advice. Most of them have told me they wish they'd settled less, spoken up more, and persevered to realize their dreams. That they should have been bolder and less cautious. That they should have approached and spoken to a specific person they wanted to get to know. Learn from those who have already traveled along life's path. Don't believe me? Ask someone in the twilight of their life what they regret more—what they did or what they didn't do?

Don't waste the opportunity your life has presented you with. You don't get a do-over. There are no replays. Stop with the coulda, woulda, shouldas. It's scary to try new things and fail. It's hard to move through self-doubt and challenges when we feel like we are alone. But the truth is, the time for action is now. Stop accepting less than you deserve. Stop playing it safe, and start playing with courage, passion, vulnerability, love, perseverance, and a hunger for what's next in life. There is no reason you can't get whatever you want in your life. So go for it.

CHAPTER 3

THE TWELVE POWER PRINCIPLES OF SOCIAL SUCCESS

"I just think that sometimes we hang onto people or relationships long after they've ceased to be of any use to either of you. I'm always meeting new people, and my list of friends seems to change quite a bit."

—*John Cleese*

I offer what I learned in my journey to successfully meet people and build relationships with the hope that these ideas will help you. Creating change takes effort, commitment, and consistency, and to battling through adversity, setbacks, doubt, failures, and the times when you feel you are completely alone can be very tough. Before we get into the action steps, I want to share some guiding power principles that will give you a great roadmap to get started.

#1: Everyone wants to belong. Beautiful people, geniuses, the rich and famous—everyone has insecurities and fears. People are sick of trying to fit in and be liked by others. But everyone wants to be loved, accepted, and cared about. If you can help others meet people, feel a sense of belonging, get out of their own negative thoughts, and just have fun, you will generate social capital quickly.

#2: Lead with giving. We live in a world of takers and people who feel entitled to things. Everyone has been taken advantage of, had their heart stomped on, been betrayed by someone they care about, or made fun of. The easiest way to break down the emotional walls this creates is to allow people to be vulnerable and feel safe around you. You can do that in seconds when giving is a part of your DNA. You allow people to share things with you because they know you can be trusted, you give them a voice, and you won't take advantage of them.

#3: Be a hub. Do you ever notice, when you go out, that most people spend their time with the people they arrived with? They rarely talk to strangers. As a social hub, you are the connecting point between people. You have an opportunity to help others make new friends and business connections, find dating or relationship opportunities, and build their network. Being a social hub is often equated with money, power, influence, or physical attractiveness, but you don't need any of these to take on this role. You just have to take action. This is the easiest and most powerful way to build social capital that enables you to have significant influence. Also, you will start to gain even more influence when you connect groups to each other, and super networkers (those with 10,000+ contacts) with each other.

#4: Network in groups. Socializing in groups, rather than one-on-one, gives you a common connection and something to discuss with new people. You can meet a lot more people— and faster—in a group environment than during one-on-one interactions. You also have the capability to connect groups to each other and to be the powerful connector to make that happen.

#5: Be open, honest, and vulnerable. Leading with these traits is crucial to people feeling comfortable around you. Sure, in an ideal world others would open up first. But that doesn't often happen. So take the lead here. You don't have to share your deepest, darkest secrets, but putting yourself out there a little bit will go a long way. Let people see who you are. You don't need to wear a mask and hide. You're awesome and it's time you believed it!

#6: Practice makes perfect. Creating a plan for your extraordinary social life takes planning, follow through, and practice. You'll need to take action to make progress. Practice your social and communication skills by committing to talk to at least 2-3 new people every day. Don't worry if you seem a little awkward or aggressive at first. If your intentions are authentic, you will come across that way more and more each time you try. Know now that failure at some point is inevitable, and every successful person fails significantly more often than they succeed. Remember, too, that failure is a great teacher.

Remember, motivation is a false god, so don't give in to it—it's not the secret ingredient for moving forward. People are always looking for motivation and complain that their lack of results is because they could not get motivated. Successful people don't wake up every day and spring into action. No one wants to do everything they need to do. They have to force themselves in many instances. Do you think every Olympic athlete wants to practice seven days a week? Of course they don't. Well, they still do it.

#7: Meeting people gets easier the more you do it. When I started out, people introduced me as "a great guy" or one of their "good friends." At first, I thought it was a lie or a joke. I mean, how could anyone I'd met only two or three times feel that way about me? Gradually, after it kept happening, I began to realize it was true. I got people to prioritize me in their life and to consider me a good friend, when we'd only met a few times, sometimes very briefly. This in turn gave me more opportunities to interact with new people because my social connections would think of me as part of their inner circle of friends and invite me to other events.

#8: Listening is a skill to be cherished. In a world where everyone talks over each other, sometimes it can be hard to get a word in, let alone realize that beneath all this chatter, people just want to be validated and heard. Who are the people you feel really listen to you? Probably trusted friends and family members, right? You can build this same trust with others by prioritizing listening over speaking. When you listen to strangers or new acquaintances, you are building rapport and strengthening bonds.

#9: You can't control critics, only your reaction to them: If you put yourself out there, you're bound to be criticized at some point. We all have someone in our life who's made us feel less-than from time to time. You've probably etched their words in your mind. Maybe it was a significant other, a boss, or a friend. Not caring what people think isn't the answer. That's being "carefree." Instead, focus on your purpose, surround yourself with people who support you, self-evaluate, and then let it go.

#10: Break the outcome-expectation cycle. When you focus on a certain expectation or outcome with others, you're bound to be disappointed or offended if someone doesn't respond to you. This, in turn, directs your focus to lack in your life, and you dwell on—and in—your current situation. If you don't expect any outcome from your social interactions, then you can be present and enjoy the moment. Rather than holding certain expectations, focus on giving and listening—these are two skills that will take you far.

#11: Make fear or worry your friend. One of the best ways to combat a fear or worry is to face it. It may never fully go away, but if you continue to battle through it, the momentum you create will be more powerful than any fear or worry you feel. You will develop the habit of always moving through fear or worry by being courageous. When I'm nervous about approaching someone, I think back to all the amazing people I met in exactly the same way. By calling up this positive memory, fear or worry subsides and I recognize the opportunity in front of me.

The worst possible outcome rarely occurs in anything we do. We can choose to be at peace or anxious in every moment. If we get upset about inconsequential things or get overwhelmed about what will happen, it prevents us from being clear in our thoughts and actions. It holds us back from enjoying the moment no matter where we are or what we are doing. In the end, everything sorts itself out.

For example, if you forget the tickets to an event, you can just go back and get them or often pull up your mobile phone and access them. Worst-case scenario, you miss a few minutes of an event. That's pretty tiny in the big scheme of life.

If you speak to a stranger, what's the worst that can happen? They walk away, say something negative to you, or throw a drink in your face. Well, I've spoken to hundreds of thousands of people, and I have never had a drink thrown in my face. I can't even count on one hand the times strangers said something rude upon our first interaction. Yes, people have walked away, but what's the impact on me? It's minimal. Sure, I missed potential opportunities, but by talking to strangers every day, I have met so many more people than I would have if I had avoided the possibility of rejection.

#12: Start asking better questions. People every day ask themselves questions that are negative, disempowering, and unproductive. This starts a daily cycle where they focus on the lack and scarcity in their lives. They also use the same thinking when positive things happen. For example, if you got laid off from a job, it actually is an opportunity to reevaluate your career. But most people start to think, "I can't believe this happened. Am I not that important to the company?" "Shouldn't I have seen that coming, or am I stupid?" "Why do bad things always happen to me?" "Can I really find a better job now?" "Doesn't this show that I really am a loser?"

Bad things often have a positive impact eventually or lead to much better opportunities. It's part of your life plan and path. Embrace it and look to use it as a springboard. What if you asked, "What does this allow me to now do?" "What does this situation make possible?" "What new career opportunities does this open up for me now?"

Accidents, tragedies, loss, and misfortune happen to all of us. We can't control everything that happens to or around us. But you can choose how you respond to what happens. Start to ask better questions that empower you.

These twelve principles have served me well over the past years, and they will help you create extraordinary and abundant relationships.

CHAPTER 4

HOW TO BUILD YOUR SOCIAL WEALTH GPS

"We are shaped by our thoughts; we become what we think. When the mind is pure, joy follows like a shadow that never leaves."

—*Buddha*

The way you interpret your life experiences through your thoughts leads to the actions you take and ultimately creates the life you are living. That makes you the master creator of your life and presents an exciting opportunity for your future. You can transform your entire life—after all, you are in control of it. Change or transformation starts from the inside, and that's a huge advantage for you.

Your success in life, including success in your relationships, is directly correlated to your psychology and thoughts. It's critical for you to master your mind, or all the work you do will be severely hampered. It's like entering a fight with both hands tied behind your back!

We perceive the world around us in the context of a story. We understand experiences and people by constructing stories around them to explain them to ourselves and others. Our stories tell us who we are, and likewise, we become defined by the stories we tell. The most powerful story that controls us is fear. Fear is connected to being loved and accepted by others. You have to realize you can't control being loved or accepted by others, and you have to let go of that thought, or it will crush your heart and soul.

Here is another way to look at it: **Something happens that has an impact on us**. For example, a man or woman we love ends a relationship with us.

We interpret the event by creating a defining story about it. Sometimes, people interpret a relationship ending as being rejected by the other person. We see ourselves as not being good enough. If we were, why would someone reject our love?

Over time, we stitch together these defining moments into the story of our life, and we play the leading role. The story unfolds as being afraid we're not good enough. We build up walls and become lonely and isolated. If we do get into another romantic situation, we might find a way to sabotage it, or we might even pick the wrong person, and we cement the story even further. The seminal moments in our lives that have pain, emotion, and hurt attached are also entangled with our romantic story. We create our identity around them. A fixed identity can hold someone back if they choose to not move past it.

Too often, we identify too much with our roles, titles, personality, possessions, and external attributes. We try too hard to be the best mother, father, brother, sister, lover, friend, employee as defined by society. We forget about who we are inside and what is it that we want. We let external forces shape us into what society wants from us and the role we are expected to play.

Once our story is written, it's difficult to erase, revise, or rewrite. If you've been told from a young age that you're not worthy, intelligent, beautiful, deserving of love—whatever it may be—and this is the story you've been living, how do you create a new, more positive story?

I understand your pain, suffering, and unhappiness. I understand the desperation you may feel at times, and that you might feel like change is just too hard to undertake. But change *is* possible. Everyone has a backstory that has shaped their lives, but it doesn't have to limit your life. If you change your story, you will change your life.

Your new story will not feel automatic at first, but as you make it a daily habit, it will become second nature and propel you forward. By creating a daily ritual process that incorporates extraordinary habits, you can support this new story and help it take root. Your new habits replace those that aren't currently serving you. A secondary function of your new habits is to maximize your productivity and efficiency, while getting you excited and fired up to take on the day.

Here is a rough outline of what your daily routine might look like:

1. When you wake up, don't hit the snooze button. Get up and take on the day.
2. As you get out of bed, tell yourself, "This is another amazing day as usual."
3. Each day, revisit your gratitude list and name three things you are grateful for. This will help you see the true abundance in your life.
4. Recite your "story." Your story, a new kind of affirmation, is a way of creating the life you want to have by telling yourself you already have it. If you contact me, and I'll send you a process to write your new story.
5. Get 20-45 minutes of exercise each day. It's also important to be energized and in good health to tackle daily challenges and opportunities.
6. Hydrate and eat a healthy breakfast to fuel yourself for your morning ahead.
7. Before getting to work each day, review your goals and long-term plan to stay focused on what you need to accomplish.
8. Write down your personal and business priorities, and what you need to accomplish them. This helps make you be clear, focused, and certain of what needs to be done. List the people you need to reach out to, to begin accomplishing your goals.

9. Recite your story at least once more in the afternoon, and use it to ward off negativity before a big meeting, a social occasion, or anytime you feel you need it.
10. Take actions each day that are in line with your story. Creating a new story about your life and reciting it daily without taking daily actions to move your life forward will hold you back.
11. Review your priority list at the end of the day, before you leave work or sign off if you work remotely. Celebrate your accomplishments and review your challenges.
12. Take five minutes each evening and be present. Take a short walk, play with your dog, or meditate.

Today, we aren't going to go through the whole life-planning process to craft your vision, purpose, story, goals, and plan. Instead, we're going to go through an abbreviated process that will take around 30 minutes to complete. Please take the time to do this exercise as it's absolutely critical to help you uncover what it is you truly want, and why do you really want it. Often we think we know what we want, but we never stop and think, "Why do I want this, and what's the motivation behind it?" Putting the *what* and *why* together is the key to getting yourself to make progress on a daily basis.

Here is a quick way to create an action plan that incorporates your goals, and a plan to accomplish them.

o **Step 1**: Write out five things you did in the last 12 months that you are proud of accomplishing. Next, circle the three that seemed the hardest. Then, write down those three things separately and the three steps that you took to make them possible. This will show you that you are successful and if you focus on something, you can make it happen.
o **Step 2**: Repeat to yourself, "I'm awesome," and pump your fist. Now, make a "W" with your arms. Raise them

above your head. Say to yourself, "I'm a winner." It's important to get your blood pumping. This creates a valuable mind-to-body connection and gets your mind into the proper state.

○ **Step 3**: Pick a date a year from today. Write, "My life would be amazing on X date if these things happened. . ."

○ **Step 4**: Write down five things that would make you feel very satisfied if you accomplished or attained them in the next year. These can be goals in any number of categories: money, career/business, health, networking, personal interests, travel, social life, relationships, dating etc.

○ **Step 5**: Now write down two to three sentences on why accomplishing each goal is important to you. In essence, you are saying to yourself, "Why do I want what I want?"

○ **Step 6**: Next, write down why you must take action toward each goal, and what will happen or how you will feel if you don't succeed. Free-associate. Don't think too long about it.

○ **Step 7**: Write, "I will be completely satisfied in my life if I accomplish these three things over the next five years." Write out what those three things are and why you want them. You can always change them up later. Write down a date five years from today.

○ **Step 8**: For your one-year plan, write out the specific steps you must take in the next 30 days to be successful in each area. Keep updating this plan every 30 days for the next year. For your five-year plan, write out the actions that need to happen this year to move you toward your goals.

○ **Step 9**: Now, take out a new piece of paper or open a new page on your computer. Write, "My life is amazing and it's going better than ever before. I am so excited about where my life is headed." Date it January 1 of next year. Write out all you accomplished in the past year. Close your eyes and see yourself on that New Year's Day. Think about how you would feel if you accomplished all your goals. Print this out and put it somewhere you can see it every single day.

o So now you have an action plan! You will want your plan to succeed more than fear, doubt and uncertainty. You will be compelled to take steps forward rather than fall backward.

CHAPTER 5

MASTERING YOUR RELATIONSHIPS: CRACKING THE SOCIAL CODE

"You can make more friends in two months by becoming interested in other people than you can in two years by trying to get other people interested in you."
—Dale Carnegie

By this point, I hope that you understand the people you meet and the relationships you make will define your life and your experiences. Mastering this area is not an option if you want to have a meaningful and extraordinary life. It is an absolute must for every area of your life: business, personal, social, etc. There are no exceptions. I'm going to show you how to crack the code.

Here is an example to illustrate this point. In July 2009, three Americans were hiking in Iraq when they unintentionally crossed the border into Iran and were arrested and accused of espionage. *In A Sliver of Light: Three Americans Imprisoned in Iran*, they discussed their experiences in captivity, their long periods of isolation, and the mental toll it took on their lives. One of the captives, Sarah Shourd, said something that really struck me: Everything in life is better when you can share with others in your life, and especially those close to you. Her time in isolation and captivity taught her that it is not possible to have a life that is fulfilling and meaningful without relationships.

In the next several chapters I am going to show you how to meet people and create extraordinary relationships for friendship, relationships, business and networking, and how to create a life that will open doors to unlimited possibilities. Many of the tools, techniques, and skills are the same for each area of life, but some are focused on what you want to create in a specific area of your life. For example, I'm dedicating a specific chapter to business and networking because there are many different strategies and actions that you can implement here.

Refer back to the core principles and concepts we already discussed, as well as the critical nature of building social capital. Before we get started, your psychology and mindset plays a huge role in your success in creating the life and relationships that you want. You can't fake or pretend to be someone you are not. Instead, take the time to cultivate the right habits that will move your life forward effortlessly and allow the world to see the exceptional person you are.

Most people will make a first impression in ten seconds or less, so how you convey your verbal and nonverbal communication upfront can decide what potential you have with the person or people you are speaking with. Most of this first impression is nonverbal communication, so smiling, eye contact, leaning in to show interest, strong and relaxed body positioning, using the power of touch, and other nonverbal actions will go a long way. We will be covering this later in the chapter.

First, I want to address a common objection that I get from people. "Well, I don't want to meet a lot of people. I just want to have a couple good friends, a relationship, and my business network will work itself out. Isn't there some quick way to do this all?" In a word: NO. Let's discuss why this is:

- If you don't take the time to understand what you want in life and why you want it, how can you ever meet the right people? Let's say one of your true passions in life is to hike because it makes you feel alive, you love being in nature, you love exercise, and it energizes you.

Why wouldn't you join a hiking organization or club? That would ensure that you meet friends, potential relationship partners and business contacts who all love to do what you do.

- You learn a lot through your experiences with people, and you learn a lot about people when you interact with them. You also learn a lot about yourself, and what you like and don't like. To really get focused, clear, and certain about what types of people you want in your life, you need to meet a *lot* of people. Two or three really good friends aren't going to just walk through your front door, nor is a dating or relationship partner. Often people settle because they live in scarcity. They are not meeting many people so their choices are very limited. They also stick with the same friends over time even if they change and their friends don't. This often holds people back. Your friendships will change over time, as you change and your friends change. Many people will come in and out of your life like busboys in a restaurant. That's a fantastic opportunity because you meet people that are traveling down the same path in life as you, and are better suited to you in your goals, interests, passions, outlook in life, etc. When you live in abundance versus scarcity, this concept isn't scary or sad; it's actually empowering and exciting.

- As I have said before, social and communication skills are learned. You have to practice them in order to master them. You will most likely have to interact with a lot more people than you currently are if you want to create a healthy, positive, successful, and rewarding skill set.

- Many people don't invest in their business network, and then when they really need it (i.e., they're laid off, fired, hate their job, want to start a business, etc.) they don't have one. There are tons of studies that show the easiest way to get a job is through networking, and you'll also have more leverage to ask for a better compensation package, salary, consulting fees, etc. Invest in your business network now and you will reap huge dividends in your life.

Next, let's discuss the psychology behind why people go out to meet other people. I think it's important to understand in order to prepare yourself for fluid, natural conversations. Also, taking a moment to go over this will help you understand why this will work for you.

I have asked thousands of people the same question. "Why do you go out to meet other people?" These are the five main responses I get in order:

1. They are trying to escape their boring and mundane lives or forget about their problems, worries, and challenges.
2. They want to be social and meet other people.
3. They are looking to meet someone of the opposite sex.
4. They are looking to network for business reasons, find new clients, or attend a business-specific event or group (i.e., lawyers association, real estate group, etc.).
5. They are looking to help others through charity work.

Remember this when you are thinking of things to say. People don't usually want to talk about work, so don't ask them about it. Stick to light and fun topics that will allow them to talk about their interests and passions. Remember, they are trying to escape whatever stress they left at the office or in life. They don't want to relive a horrible day at work in their conversation with you.

This is especially true in business settings. You can stand apart from everyone else if you take a different approach. In a business context, almost everyone will ask you, "What do you do?" and "What company do you work for?" Start with non-work related topics and then transition into someone's current challenges and how you can help them. We will discuss this more in the subsequent chapter on business and networking.

Here are other big DON'Ts:

- DON'T talk about religion, politics, or anything controversial.
- DON'T be negative.
- DON'T ask the getting-to-know-you questions, like where are you from, do you have siblings, etc. It's boring. Be creative!
- DON'T be a know-it-all and try to show someone up. No one likes to be embarrassed by someone else in public.
- DON'T give advice. It comes off as arrogant and it doesn't go over well. People can take it as criticism.
- DON'T argue. If someone disagrees with you, just say, "I can see where you are coming from." Even if you win the argument, you will leave someone with a bad feeling about you, and everyone else around you will see that you have to prove you are right at someone else's expense. Do you want to be right or happy?
- DON'T dominate the conversation and keep talking. Engage the other person. My rule of thumb is to talk 30% and listen 70%. You have two ears and one mouth for a reason!
- DON'T be overeager in your conversation and try to agree to agree, or smile too much and nod at everything the other person says. It will be very off-putting to the other person and may seem fake.
- DON'T panic if there is a silence or lull in a conversation. Silences happen all the time between good friends. Stay confident and positive, and don't start overanalyzing. Return to a topic you talked about before or switch gears to something else, and ask a question. You can also make a joke: "Well, that was a conversation stopper!" or "There is not much someone

can say to that. Ha!" or "Yeah, that's an interesting point. What do you think about X?" Finally, exchange contact information (we will cover that later) and graciously excuse yourself.

- DON'T freak out if someone says to you, "You are being so quiet." Many times people are just making sure you are OK or they are not boring you. This also can stem from the nonverbal communication you are showing. Don't get defensive, lose your confidence, or shrink away.

It's no fun to be put on the spot about an upcoming election, cornered by someone ranting about their boss, or asked the same questions you've been asked a thousand times. So be smart and steer clear of these rookie mistakes. Here's the good news: If you want to know what to talk about, or if you lose your train of thought, all you have to do is listen to people. That's it. They'll give you cues for the next question to ask. People love to talk about themselves, and people rarely feel really listened to. *You* can be that person who listens and increase your social capital in the process.

And remember to take the lead in the conversation. Don't wait around for someone to start it or continue it. Most people have social anxiety and/or lack of confidence in themselves. By taking the lead it allows them to get comfortable with you and takes the burden off them of having to think of things to say or questions to ask.

Here are critical points to understand about how to create more positive outcomes in your conversations and not run out of things to say:

- People focus way too much on what to say and trying to say the right thing. Research has found your delivery is much more important than content in building rapport, especially in initial interactions. It's not what you say, it's how you say it. People feed off your emotions, energy, and vibe, because you are projecting your frame and feelings to them. They feel and see your charisma and magnetism when you do this correctly, and when you are being yourself. They are attracted to you and want to speak to you because of your nonverbal communication, confidence, strong positive convictions, and belief about who you are and what you want.

- If you are talking to a young child, you might say whatever you think will make them laugh. But when you are talking with adults, you may start to judge yourself and filter your comments. Stop overanalyzing. Keep the conversation light and fun. You may not always have the most interesting thing to say, but people know you are just being yourself and saying what's on your mind. People are attracted to and engaged by that type of confidence and vibe. And they will value what you say because it is coming from you.

- Being present in your conversations is huge. When you're not looking at the person you're speaking to (i.e., making poor eye contact) and instead you're busy looking around to see what's going on across the room, you're creating a lose-lose situation. The person or people you are talking to get the signal that you aren't interested in what they are saying and that you want to be somewhere else. So you've blown that interaction. Focus on the present moment and be engaged. Practice this! You can always excuse yourself and go talk to other people, but don't lose out on opportunities when you don't need to.

- Engage in a conversation, rather than simply waiting your turn to speak. When you are busy trying to think of the next thing to say, you are not really listening to the other person. This goes back to trying to impress or get someone to like us because we don't feel like we are good enough. We try to rack our brains for something clever or interesting because we feel that's necessary to keep the conversation going. But when we don't worry about what comes next and we're present, true connections with others really start. All you're doing is having a good time, just enjoying the moment you're sharing with this other person. Just stay in the moment and let the conversation flow out of you.

- People are interested in what you are saying because you are interested in it. When you meet people, they want to get to know you, how you see the world, and so forth. They don't want you to try to be someone else or try to impress them. That's not being your authentic self. If you are passionate, positive, and excited about what you are saying, you will be able to transfer your current state of being to the other person. People will lose themselves or flow directly into the positive emotions and conversation. I've found that when you use humor and laugh at things you find really funny, other people get sucked into it and laugh too. The same thing happens when you talk about something you feel passionate about. The other person is naturally drawn in because you are being real, authentic, emotional, and sharing something about you. They are getting a glimpse of who you really are. But if you try to force humor to get someone to laugh, they'll know this isn't really you and they will be put off. That's why using canned lines or routines doesn't work. Finally, this can also work the opposite way and kill the interaction if someone is negative. You will transfer negative energy and repel the other person.

- Remember, everyone has some level of social anxiety. Even the most socially skilled people don't feel 100% at ease all the time. People fear they have nothing of value to share or offer, and they get it in their head to allow negativity to creep in. So make people feel relaxed around you by being positive, present, nonjudgmental, and excited about them. You will allow them to feel free around you, like they can open up. The next time you are out, try smiling, keeping good eye contact, asking questions, and being engaged, and see what happens with your conversations. You will be amazed at how much better they go.

- Having confidence in yourself is absolutely critical for every interaction you have. In conversations, you have value in everything you say because it comes from you. Since you are the source, it is awesome. When you don't believe that, you give off the vibe and energy that you are not secure in yourself...and that's not attractive or engaging. Remember, your uniqueness is your power.

- Giving to, helping, and inspiring others without wanting anything back is the easiest and quickest way to eliminate or minimize social anxiety. Why? Because you don't have expectations about what you need to accomplish to consider it a success. If you go out to meet someone of the opposite sex, and you go home with no results, you'll get frustrated. If you went out to have fun, make others laugh, enjoy your time with friends or meet new friends, you take all that pressure off yourself and enjoy the time you are spending doing whatever you are doing. You are not on a mission to get something from someone else. You give to others by giving the gift of listening, making them smile, introducing them to one of your friends or a stranger, etc. Giving has nothing to do with resources; it has to do with being resourceful. Throw your agendas in the trash, and go live life without having a scorecard to judge your success or failure. You will be amazed how much more goes positively for you, and how many more people want to interact and be in your life.

- It's really important to match the communication styles of the people you are interacting with in order to build rapport. If you are with someone who is an extrovert and outgoing, you should be excitable, playful, and outspoken. If you are with an introvert who is more quiet then ratchet down your communication and interactions. If you mismatch styles, it can be an immediate turn-off and the interaction won't go anywhere. Ask yourself, how fast or slow does your companion talk? What's their body language like? Do they speak loudly or softly? In essence, you are mirroring their style and showing them you are in sync with them and sensitive to the way they prefer to interact. This doesn't mean being someone you are not.

Now let's get into what you can say to start any conversation, anywhere. Here are a few easy conversation starters:

- "Happy Friday, how's your week going?"
- (If you have a beverage) "Cheers! What's going on?"
- "Tell me what you are most excited about in your life right now..." (love this one)
- "So what projects are you working on that you are most passionate about?" or "What are you most passionate about in your life outside of work?"
- "How did you get started in that (whatever their job/career is)?"

Alternatively, you can ask:

- "How's your night going?" or "What's happening?" or "What's on your agenda for the weekend?" or "What did you do this week (or weekend)?"

And you never want to forget:

- "How's everything?"

If you're at an event:

- "What brings you here tonight?" or "How are you involved with this organization?"

A great catchall phrase to use:

- "That's fantastic. Tell me more..."

Asking questions will get people talking, and people love to share their experiences. People also love to share their opinions. Many people don't have anyone who truly listens to them, so if you are that person, that can help build rapport quickly. Often, our best listeners are our closest friends. So by listening, you are acting like a person's close friend, and someone is likely to think of you like that, which is another reason why this is a powerful tool for rapport building.

Here are some good opinion questions:

- "Hey, do you know any great restaurants around here?"
- "Where do you like to go out in the city?" or "Have you been to any new hot spots in the city lately?"
- "Do you know any great organizations I should check out?"
- "What upcoming events are you excited about?"
- Or just, "What do you think about..."

You put that person in the position to be an expert, and you value you them enough to ask for their opinion. Plus, you are actually listening to them versus talking. Most people talk significantly more than they listen because they are trying to "sell" themselves and get validation or approval from someone else. Validate and approve yourself and you move past a major obstacle so many people get caught up in.

Also, it is powerful when you give people positive feedback, praise, or a compliment, but only when it is genuine. If you find out someone got a new job, congratulate them. If you hang out with someone often and they make you laugh, tell them. If you run into someone and they are wearing something striking, mention it. If someone makes a good suggestion or idea, tell them. The key here is to be genuine and specific about the comment you are about to make.

Here is what a typical conversation might look like:

- "How's your week going?"
- Let's say they mention they went to a concert. "That sounds like a lot of fun. Tell me more. Are you a big music fan?" You could follow up with any of the following: "What are your favorite bands?" "Where do you like to see bands?" "Do you play an instrument?"
- Interject some commentary about what they are saying, and also if you have an opinion on music. Don't try to impress someone or lie. Just be yourself and add to the conversation.
- Also, point out any commonalities you have with someone else. It's good to try to establish things in common to build rapport. You don't have to go overboard here or try too hard. If something comes up that is genuine, point it out.
- Then end the conversation by exchanging contact information (we will cover this later) and/or just say, "It was great to meet you, I have a few other people I need to speak with." Or "I need to join my friends, why don't you come over here and meet them." Or "I am getting a drink, would you like anything?" Then you can go get them a drink, bring it back, and move on.

A conversation is simple: start it, engage the other person and build rapport, keep it going for few minutes, and then leave them thinking you are great person that they want to get to know better. It really just boils down to that.

What about approaching groups of people? These openers work well:

- "What occasion are you all celebrating tonight?"
- "What brings you all together today?"
- You can also just use the openers we discussed earlier, and when you ask them what they are doing for the week or weekend, they will mention the group activity.
- If you find out it is a bachelorette party, you can say, "I'm the entertainment for the evening!" Don't be afraid to show a little humor.

And always focus on listening to and helping the other person first!

Bantering

Bantering is a fun but powerful way to have conversations with people. It is using humor in a positive way to help people escape. And it's a great way create positive tension. You can also use this in a business or networking setting, though you will need to tone it down.

Why does this work so well? When you tease a person and you're willing to take risks in conversation, it shows that you have NO FEAR.

For men, being Mr. Nice Guy keeps the conversation safe, but it also spells *major fear of rejection.* Women are very perceptive, and they don't usually respond too well to this. But when you boldly tease a woman and make conversation fun for her, you actively demonstrate you don't have FEAR. You're not concerned about saying the wrong thing.

More importantly, you're not broadcasting your fear of LOSING her, before you've even ATTRACTED her. Bantering works on men as well, so women, it's time to chat it up!

There are two basic ways to engage in friendly banter:

1) The first is a form of a question based on selective hearing. "Did you just ask me…?" It doesn't matter what someone says; interject to lead to the outcome you want. "Did you just ask for my phone number?"
2) The next is a statement. It doesn't matter what someone says, it is about what you believe they said. "If you wanted my phone number, you should have just asked for it." "If you wanted to talk to me, you should have approached me a long time ago. I don't bite!"

Other examples:

- If you're with a buddy and someone asks, "How do you two know each other?" Your response: *Prison.* They may say, "How do you *really* know each other?" You can then tell the real story of how you met, but say the prison story is much funnier to tell.
- "Did you just ask to buy me champagne?"
- If someone asks you how you are doing, you can say, "I'm feeling rather sexy (or awesome)."

Banter works much better when you do inner work regularly to gain more self-confidence and create a better vibe. I also recommend practicing banter with your friends and people you see often (i.e., with the barista at Starbucks, a hotel clerk, etc.) before you use it on strangers. Also remember to be respectful of others and not a jerk. Finally, if someone isn't playing along with your banter, just say you were joking around, and drop it immediately.

Here are some additional tips that will help you start a conversation with anyone, anywhere:

Tip #1: Before you go out in public, whether it's to start your day, on a coffee break, lunch, happy hour, meeting, event, etc., do at least part of your "story." Or you can create something quick that gets you in the right mind frame. Here is an example:

"I always get excited to speak to new people, and I feel courageous when I do it. I have amazing conversations with people, and I leave them wanting to speak to me more. People love to be around me, and they find it fascinating to interact with me. They always look forward to seeing me again, and we exchange information with a plan to follow up and meet again. With every new interaction, I feel inspired, motivated, and alive! I just want to raise my arms and say 'YES!'"

Remember to visualize success and get physically excited. You can at least pump your fist, even if in public. Who cares who sees you? They won't even remember seeing you do that five minutes from now. But creating physical excitement can make a major difference for you!

Tip #2: I want to discuss why confidence is very important in your interactions. As you are improving and practicing your social and communications skills, you may not feel confident all the time. When I was starting out, I thought, how would someone who has unflappable confidence ask a question? How would they stand? How would they project themselves? Stand confidently with your chest out (don't slouch) and legs shoulder-width apart, and take up a little bit of space. Have a confident, positive tone in your voice. Be self-assured with your hand gestures and body motions. Don't cross your arms, and instead have your palms pointing up, which signals that you are open and inviting others to engage with you.

Something else that really helped me: *I assumed I had rapport with people immediately.* I started treating them like an old friend. That helped me relax more, and released anxiety because I didn't need to try to get approval or any validation. I already had it in my mind that they enjoyed spending time with me and liked me.

You can even picture yourself as a celebrity, successful

business person or someone famous who projects confidence. Try whatever works for you.

Tip #3: If you want to practice your speaking skills and become a more dynamic and confident speaker, go to Toastmasters (toastmasters.org). There are Toastmaster organizations in more than 120 countries worldwide, designed to help you get much better at speaking in front of others, and be better at coming up with things to say. You can join a local improv group where you will act out scenes and have to think on your feet. Finally, you can download or play a free-association game with friends to help come up with things to say on the spot.

Research shows that people rate delivery as more important than the actual content. So these groups and activities can go a long way in improving your interactions with others.

Learning from others, finding very social and outgoing people to hang out with, and modeling off of successful coaches that have a large network of people and proven social and communications skills is very powerful and can significantly help you move forward.

Social and communications skills need to be practiced daily and mastered to get the life you truly want. You can find a way to make this happen.

Tip #4: Here some additional ways to spice up your conversations to make better connections with others.

- Mirror statements: These are statements that basically rephrase what the other person said, along with a little bit of active listening. If the other person says, "I just had an amazing vacation. I feel so relaxed right now!" You would say, "Wow, you look very relaxed. What did you do on your vacation?"
- Assuming statements: People love to get positive

feedback and hear what other people think. "That's very courageous of you to quit your job and follow your dreams. You seem like a person who is very driven and knows what they want in life."

- Bridging statements: Sometimes you are talking with someone and they don't leave you much to go on or where to take the conversation. You can take a word they use or an idea and go in another direction. You: "How's your night going?" Them: "Good." You: "Speaking of good, have you tried any of the new restaurants that are popping up all over town?" Them: "No, which ones?" You: "I went to XYZ restaurant and they had the best sushi. What are your favorite types of foods?"

- Situation statements or questions: "What brought you out tonight?" "How long have you been playing XYZ sport?" "This is a pretty great party, I'm meeting a lot of fantastic people." "Do you know what the name of this song is?" "That was a great movie. Have you seen any other great movies lately?"

- Why questions: Instead of asking boring questions such as, "What's new?" "What do you do for a living?" start asking why people are doing what they are doing. "Why did you decide to go on vacation to Europe?" "Why did you choose your profession?"

Tip #5 There are always more "fish in the sea" and other people to talk to. You must accept that not every conversation is going to go well, and some just fizzle out and you have to move on. That's life. Sometimes you may not be 100% feeling your best, and sometimes the other person isn't. You can't control the other person, and if you live your life trying to convince everyone to like you, you are going to burn out and really be challenged in all your relationships.

If it starts to fizzle, just say, "It was great to meet you, I am going to say hi to some other people," or "It was fantastic to meet you, have a wonderful night," or "I'm going to take off now…"

Practice and repetition will play a big role in the success of your personal and business conversations.

Tip #6: *I can't stress enough how important being vulnerable and candid with people is, and how quickly you build relationships with people when you are.* Not long ago I was out and ran into an acquaintance of mine. She looked upset and distressed. I asked her if something was wrong and she said she was OK. I could have left it at that, but I didn't. Instead I decided to try and create opportunity for her to share what was going on. So I shared a quick story about a couple challenges I was having in my life. Because I created a bridge by being open, vulnerable, and candid, she was able to bring up a painful story of abuse that had happened to her in the past that was finally starting to resurface. So we sat down and talked for a while. I mainly just listened. After that, we were able to join some other people, and her mood immediately perked up. Sometimes people need someone to talk to in order to move forward. Be that person!

Next, I want to tackle head on some common roadblocks that people bring up and how to overcome them.

Roadblock: Fear and Pain of Rejection

People often say to me, "Jason, I can't go up and speak to a stranger. They will reject me or not want to continue talking to me." This is exactly the negative mindset so many people have their entire lives. They miss out on so many people and opportunities because they sabotage themselves by creating a fear and pain in their mind that isn't based on facts or reality. I've spoken to a large number of people over the years about their fears, and I've found fear is a self-made prison.

I ask people, "Have you ever have been rejected by a person in a way that truly hurt you?" Everyone says yes to this. Then I ask them, "Can you think of three people who have done this?

Five people?" Most people identify between three to seven people who have truly rejected them. You do find sometimes this number can be as high as 10, but it rarely ever goes higher than that. Then I ask, "How many people have you encountered in your life so far who have been patient and positive, or at least neutral in how they interacted with you? Would you say at least several hundred? What about a thousand? What about several thousand?" Most people say at least a thousand people. So let's do the math here for a moment. Out of a thousand people a person has encountered, only three to seven have truly rejected them. That's a really small number! So people are being controlled by a fear that doesn't really have a foundation. We focus so much on the potential rejection that we magnify the probability that we'll be rejected.

Change takes work, effort, and daily commitment. It's not going to be easy, but it's also not impossible, and it will happen if you take action to make the progress necessary. Fear doesn't end when you commit to change. But those who stay on course focus on what will happen if they complete change. Perhaps they will lose weight and it will give them more energy and allow them to live their life more fully. Maybe someone wants to start their own business, and this will give them the flexibility to work from home and spend more time with their family or provide additional financial freedom. Change can be embraced and fun. Challenges can bring a new hunger for life and things to look forward to. So it's critical to foster the perspective of positivity instead of retreating to negativity and staying in your comfort zone.

People also fear the outcome of change. What if I don't accomplish this? What if I fail? What if I can't do it? What if I do all this work and nothing is any different? What if the grass is not truly greener when I do this? Instead of that viewpoint, what if we looked at the positive and empowered ourselves, and thought about what would be possible if it worked out. What if I made that happen in my life? What would that enable me to do? You can direct your mind to focus on what you can accomplish. Instead of running from pain and suffering that you might experience, change your mindset. Get clear, focused, and certain on what you want, and why. Ask yourself why you are not progressing faster in your life? What's really holding you back? So if you focus on the positive, you can master your mind and move past your fears.

Bottom line here is you miss 100% of the opportunities you don't take. There is a huge cost for inaction. By not taking action, typically people start to rationalize not doing something, and hope that it will all work out. Hope is not an effective life strategy. "My job isn't that bad; it will eventually get better." "My relationship isn't that bad, I guess." These situations tend to worsen over time, not get better.

We underestimate our ability to take on challenges and risks in our lives. We let self-doubt sabotage our ability to rise to potential opportunities. I see this in my clients all the time. Then I give them a task they don't think they can do, and almost always they succeed. And they tell me afterward, there really was no risk at all. They didn't have to fear for their life, safety, or livelihood.

Ask yourself:

- Why am I focusing more on what I have to lose than what I have to gain in meeting people?
- What will my behavior and inaction cost me in the next year? Next two years? Next 10 years?
- What am I underestimating in my ability to meet people?
- If I had all the confidence and courage in the world, exuded positivity and happiness, and believed in myself, what would be possible in meeting people?
- Your answers are going to point to the much bigger and more meaningful life you could be living.

Roadblock: Perfect Thing to Say

I get this question almost every single week: What's the one thing I can say to get results? People feel like there is a magic line that could change every interaction if they just knew it. Well, I'm going to burst your bubble right now.

First, nothing can replace your nonverbal communication. So focus more on creating confidence, positivity, excitement, and happiness, and practice your social and communication skills daily. There are no words or techniques that will make up for your insecurities, fears, negativity, etc. People will see through you and what you are doing. People want to be around others who are positive, happy, and excited in their lives. They face enough negativity and struggles already, and they don't need another one to deal with.

Stop wasting time looking for shortcuts and master your own mind in order to successfully move forward in meeting people and building extraordinary relationships.

Secondly, your opening line or conversation isn't that important; it's more about what you can do after that and your follow-up.

Remembering Names

When you're meeting a lot of people, how can you remember every person's name? There are lots of schools of thought on this, but I've found the best way is to repeat their name back to them, and then to introduce them to another person using their first name. When you run into them again wherever you may be, make sure to say their name once more, maybe in parting, to commit it to memory. Saying someone's name out loud makes an immediate association.

Next, try to connect their name with something visual. So if you met someone named Bill, think of them and a dollar bill. If you meet someone named Michael, I think of Michael Jordan the basketball player. If you can't think of anything, picture them with a huge nametag across their chest with their name on it.

People love it when you remember details about them, and

their name tops the list. You also want to try and remember anything else that comes up about a new person that is important. I sometimes jot quick notes in my smartphone after I exchange information with someone else so I can make sure I don't forget something we discussed.

Finally, let's cover nonverbal communication, and some simple things you can use to leverage this powerful part of human interactions.

Body Language, Positioning, and Delivery Matter

Amy Cuddy of Harvard Business School recently discussed in *Harvard* magazine how to appear strong and confident, and why being the alpha matters. She cited a study by two researchers at Columbia University who measured the hormone levels of 42 subjects, placed them in two high-power or low-power poses for a minute per pose, then remeasured their hormone levels 17 minutes later. Each subject was offered the chance to gamble, rolling dice to double a $2 stake. The results surprised the researchers: even spending just two minutes in a high- or low-power pose caused testosterone to rise and cortisol to decrease, or vice versa. High-power subjects were also more likely to gamble, a behavior associated with dominant individuals, and they reported feeling more powerful.

Nonverbal cues, body language, and physical positioning all impact how we are perceived by others. You have one opportunity to make a first impression and build strong rapport when you meet someone. You do not have time to waste in your face-to-face interactions. You need to quickly understand what someone else is really feeling and thinking and how you can influence them—something you have control over if you have control over your body language, nonverbal cues, and expressions.

So-called "micro expressions" are the most reliable form of body language and nonverbal communication, and are astonishingly accurate indicators of someone's emotional state.

This is why the FBI and CIA have been investing heavily in leveraging micro expressions in threat detection and interrogation. Micro expressions are subtle muscle movements of the face that last a half second or less (aka, partial facial expressions). You can see them in action on the show *Lie to Me*. You might be surprised how powerful nonverbal interactions are in your relationships with others. According to Cuddy, venture-capital pitches get funded not because of their content but because of the nonverbal cues of those pitching. It's more about "how comfortable and charismatic you are. The predictors of who actually gets the money are all about how you present yourself." In one study, strong predictors of success included calmness, passion, eye contact, and lack of awkwardness.

Because people tend to mirror each other, nonverbal states, like confidence, can be infectious. This mirroring effect increases social cohesiveness and connection. Take a smile, for example. A natural true smile, which is signaled by muscle engagement around the eyes, causes the smiler to feel happier. In turn, someone who sees this smile feels happier and involuntarily mirrors the smile.

Mirroring is a powerful tool, and you do it by mirroring the other person's vocal tone and patterns, body movements, mannerisms, and expressions. It's an easy way to build rapport. And you can tell if it is working because the other person will begin to match your actions. If you raise and lower your arms, they will as well. If you start nodding, they will nod back. However, don't use it as a manipulative tool to try and get something. Only use it if you truly want to build a connection with another person.

Negative body language can also be mirrored. For example, if cross your arms, signaling that you are closed off, the other person may do a similar maneuver.

Remember, your confidence level and *how* you deliver information greatly outweighs *what* you say. A common mistake people make is placing too much importance on what to say. This can make someone sound scripted, Cuddy says. It's far more effective, she notes, to "come into a room, be trusting, connect with the audience wherever they are, and then move them with you."

Here are some other important body-language signals that can help you in your interactions:

- A powerful rapport technique, when done correctly, is touching. For most people this is a handshake, and sometimes a hug if two people know each other well enough (you can hug someone you don't know if you can calibrate well enough). I think a great place to touch someone is on the outside of their elbow. It shows a little more intimacy, doesn't invade their personal space, and can help to get someone to be more talkative. In a business setting, I'll do it if someone is an extrovert because that matches more of that style, and I won't do it if I can tell someone is an introvert. Also, in personal and social interactions, if someone touches your elbow back, you know you are in sync with them. Don't go and touch their elbow a second time if you don't get some touching back from them. It is a sign that you may not be in sync or that they are not touchy-feely!

- You can tell a smile is genuine if you can see wrinkles around the eyes. That shows that true rapport building is happening and that the person is truly interested in what you are saying. If you see a smile that is asymmetrical, where one side is higher than the other, it shows contempt. That person believes they are superior to you or that they know more than you. If someone has a sideways smile with their eyebrows going up, it means they are interested in you or what you are saying. If their eyebrows are down, it indicates disagreement or hostility.

- When shaking someone's hand, make sure your hand is

parallel to the floor and squeeze your companion's hand slightly harder than they squeeze yours, while keeping eye contact. This shows you are assertive, friendly, and engaged. Don't shake with your palms facing the floor, or so that the other person's palm is facing the sky. This is a power move to show superiority. A weak handshake signals a submissive, insecure personality. A very hard handshake indicates aggression. Rise, if seated, to shake someone's hand and make sure your shoulders are aligned with the other person's.

- Eye contact is important in any conversation. You don't want to be the one who breaks eye contact first because it shows tension, concern about what people are thinking, and a lack of confidence. You can practice this several ways. In front of a mirror, relax your eye muscles so you don't look like you are staring at someone. Next, ask a friend to hold eye contact with you for several minutes without any facial expression. This will help you feel more relaxed and get you used to holding someone's gaze for a longer period of time. Here are a couple things to watch out for with eye contact:
  - If someone looks away for the majority of your conversation, it typically indicates disinterest.
  - If someone maintains eye contact 60% to 70% of the time, you have good rapport with that person.
  - If you see someone's pupils getting larger, it is a sign of deep interest or love.
- With your hands, you want to be careful that you don't have clenched fists as this is a sign of anger. Holding your palms so they face the other person shows that you are being open and inclusive; it's a welcome sign to others to approach you. Here are a few other pointers about your hands:
  - Pointing your finger indicates aggressive behavior.
  - Steepled hands means you are very self-confident,

bordering on being a person who believes they know it all.

- o If someone has their hands on their wrists, it is an indication of frustration or trying to maintain self-control. If their hands are resting on their elbows, it shows an even higher level of frustration.
- o Putting your hands on the table can be a sign of agreement. You need to consider the overall context to be sure.
- o If someone has their hands on their hips, it is a sign of aggressive behavior.
- o If someone has their hands in their pockets with the thumbs outside, it is a sign of sexual interest or aggressiveness.
- o If someone is touching their nose, it typically means they are being deceitful. If they are scratching the side of their nose, they are becoming very angry.

- If someone's legs are aligned with yours, it is an indication of interest in what you are saying. If your companion's legs are pointing away, you have lost the other person's attention. If someone is tapping their feet, it typically shows they are bored or they wish you would just stop talking. Here are a few other things to pay attention to:
  - o If someone is crossing their legs, it is a sign they are closed off and not receptive to you.
  - o If someone is sitting and has their legs crossed, with an ankle resting on a knee and with their hands on that leg, it indicates they are ready to argue or try to be competitive with you.
  - o If someone's ankles are crossed, it indicates they are holding back information from you.
  - o If someone has their hands on both knees, it shows they are interested and engaged.

o   If someone's shoulders are aligned with yours, it
    shows they are interested and that you've made
    a connection with them. If someone's arms are
    crossed or they shrug, typically it means they are
    closed off and disinterested.

There is a lot more to body language, but this is a good
overview of what to look for in your conversations and what
not to do.

CHAPTER 6

ADVANCED SOCIAL WEALTH STRATEGIES

"First, you have to be visible in the community. You have to get out there and connect with people. It's not called net-sitting or net-eating. It's called *networking*. You have work at it."

—*Dr. Ivan Misner*

Remember what I said in the beginning of this book about groups? Becoming a part of a group allows you to meet more people, experience more, learn more about yourself and others, and create mutually supportive relationships. I'm talking about the hugely important concept of building your social capital that we covered earlier. I want to discuss in this chapter how you can meet more people, while creating your social capital and/or leveraging it to help you.

As I mentioned before, there are great places to meet people and not-so-great places. I wanted to address a major reason why that is. A lot of people who are out and about in settings such as bars, clubs, and restaurants aren't there to be social. They are out to spend time with their friends, talk about a work situation, discuss some personal drama, and so forth. Those individuals are not interested in meeting you, and no matter what you do or say, your chances of having a conversation are pretty low.

Next, many men and women suffer from social anxiety; they're uncomfortable approaching someone, they don't know what to say or how to interact. Yet they keep going into the toughest situations: bars, clubs, restaurants, high-end hotels, and the like. In these environments, it's impossible to break the bad habits that are pushing them further down their rabbit hole of despair.

I'll say it one more time: Social skills are *learned behaviors.* This is huge! Anyone can learn to be great at approaching and speaking to others. It takes practice, along with the right mindset and other tools. If you don't go out and practice, you won't get any better. If you want a different result, *you've got to change your thoughts, behaviors, and actions.*

So go to lower-stress and easier environments to practice and feel more comfortable, where you can create more successful interactions and build your confidence, along with the evidence that you *can* do it. Through this process you will become much better at speaking to anyone—anywhere— because you will have gained some level of mastery and have much more confidence than you had before, along with just being more comfortable approaching and speaking with people.

You can keep trying it the hard way and stay stuck in your same frustrating social patterns, or you can try something different and create new, more effective interactions. Engage with people everywhere you go, and practice with anyone, anytime, anywhere. If I am at Whole Foods, I'll say hi to other people shopping and just make quick small talk. I use whatever environment I am in to practice. I also speak with cashiers, baristas, store owners, chefs, waiters, valets, etc. This really helped me gain mastery over my social and communication skills quickly because I just didn't do it every once in a while or on the weekends. I did it every single day as much as I could. Sure, many of the interactions didn't lead to anything, but I was always learning and making progress.

Key Things to Keep in Mind When Meeting People

The key to being successful in meeting people and building relationships much faster than others is cementing the thought in your head that making *other* people successful will unlock limitless opportunities for every area of your life. So remember to give first without expecting anything back. There are very few people that do this, and most people rarely, if ever, meet someone like this, so you will stand out. You will widen, deepen, and expand your social capital at a very fast rate, and you will see your sphere of influence in the world around you grow.

You will find that people will be willing to do almost anything for you, and that will help you create extraordinariness in every area of your life. The people you help will be rooting for you to be successful.

Here are a few things to keep in mind:

- Make people feel special, and they will treat you as a very close friend even if you have only known them for a very short time.
- People want to be appreciated and feel good about themselves. It fulfills a person's basic need to belong and feel significant in the eyes of other people.
- You can gain power and influence very quickly if you become invaluable to others by helping them. People who have never even met you will know about you and want to meet you.
- Creating extraordinary relationships is 20% meeting people, 80% is what comes after that. Focus on following up, building the relationship, and finding ways to stay in touch.

Let's discuss the first advanced strategy on where to meet people.

Interest Groups

Developing new skill sets, playing a sport, or taking time out to have fun and do something you enjoy is sometimes hard to make work with your likely busy schedule. But in order for people to feel truly alive, they need to cultivate and explore their interests and passions, and try new things. One way to do this is by participating in group activities. What's great is that you also get to meet people who have a hobby/interest in common with you, and that makes it much easier to meet everyone in that group/organization quickly. Imagine how hard it would be to find groups of people randomly who like to ski, salsa dance, read books, or play music. Also, I think there is something to be said about having something to look forward to and be excited about. Every week or every month, you will have something to do just for fun. Joining these groups really helped me early on, and I was involved in running a book club, went to a film club, and played coed flag football in Dallas. I made a lot of fantastic friends and really looked forward to seeing them every week.

What if you don't know what you want to do or don't have really any current interests? Pick something! Try going to an art class, an indoor rock climbing class, playing volleyball or kickball, etc. If you don't like it, then you don't have to go back, and maybe you'll have a better sense of what you *would* like. For example, maybe you didn't like the art class because you really wanted to talk to more people. Well, now you learned something that will help you decide what to try next.

Finally, the golf course is the place where a lot of networking and business deals get done. It is a great sport to learn to play because of the connections you can make on and off the golf course. You can join a country club, golf association, or participate in the myriad of golf charity outings that go on year round.

Politics

For those who are interested, this is a way to meet likeminded people or be involved with candidates that represent your views. There are a ton of organizations, from the official parties, to young professional groups, think tanks, the candidates themselves, etc. There are great advantages to getting involved in local politics. Remember, today's unknown politician can easily be a future mayor or congressperson, who would be a powerful person to have in your network.

Charities and Nonprofits

I am a huge proponent of going to charity benefits, nonprofits, and cultural events as well as networking and business events, which we'll cover later in the book. Most of these organizations have monthly or quarterly events, and some have a gala event once a year. Charity and nonprofit happy hour events are really great because they are usually held in the middle of the week when there are not many other events happening, and they are typically inexpensive (i.e., $10-$15 with a drink and sometimes appetizers). You can go out for just a couple of hours in the early evening and typically be home before nine o'clock.

Many of the people going to these events are very well connected and very social (think VIPs in your city) young professionals and business executives, and they have large networks of their own that you can tap into. People are also much more open to meeting others, and much less guarded, at these events, as we discussed earlier. And the setting makes it easier to break the ice in initial conversations, just as in interest groups. This makes it easier to meet people. Their defense mechanisms are much lower than those of the people you will meet at bars, clubs, and other like places. Part of that is because people are coming together for a specific reason and some people at the event know each other. By working the room, you can meet many people in a very brief time and exchange contact information.

As you continue to go to these events, you will start recognizing the same people. Why? Because many people are involved in several charities and nonprofit organizations, and they go to their events regularly. Plus, they are often socially mobile professionals who will be out and about in your city doing social things.

Soon they will start responding to you like they've run into an old friend. Chances are, they will actually be seeing you more than they see a lot of their very good friends. So this is a great opportunity to build new relationships and expand your network quickly.

You'll also find that some people may have been associated with the same organizations for years but have barely spoken to each other. *You* can help them connect and make new connections for yourself, and that's an important opportunity. It's a way to really take your life to the next level!

If you find a group that does something you feel passionate about, take it to next level and volunteer. Volunteering is a great way to meet more of the people in an organization. Just contact the organizer and say, "Hey, if you need any help, I'm available." The organizer typically will introduce you to other volunteers, so you will quickly get to know people involved in the organization.

If you have a high level of social anxiety, volunteer before the event starts so you can get used to the environment and meet a few people in the organization. Just go to the website or the Facebook page and see who is in charge of membership and events. Contact them and say that you would like to volunteer for their next event. I'd say in the email that you'd like to work the check-in table at the start of the event. In many instances, you can also go to the event for free if you volunteer (even an expensive gala event). If you work the check-in table, you can meet many of the people at the event as they come in. This makes it easier to work the room later because you will have already met them once and built some initial rapport. I told you this was easy!

Finally, you can really enhance your network and meet some amazing people if you take on a leadership role in a charity or nonprofit organization by helping with their major events, or being on their board of advisors. But make sure you are fully behind their cause and it is something you are passionate about. Don't participate to add it to your resume and be a social climber.

How Do You Find Charity, Nonprofit, and Other Events?

It is critical that you spend time building your list. I suggest you use a spreadsheet and keep track of all the events, and put them in your calendar. Remember, you can't attend events you don't know about.

Your local newspaper or independent weekly will have listings or advertisements for upcoming charity, nonprofit, and other events such as restaurant openings, fashion shows, and lectures. You can also use Google, searching your city and terms like *charity events, young professionals, gala events,* and so forth. You can also take a look at the websites for local nonprofits, museums, symphonies, theaters, and other cultural organizations. Google *philanthropy* or *charity calendars* as well. Sign up for each charity or nonprofit's newsletter and "Like" their Facebook page to get updates on their events. Get on local bloggers' email lists for food, fashion, music, nightlife, and charity, and sign up for online daily publications such as *Culture Map, Urban Daddy,* and others. Finally, when you are at an event, ask people there what they recommend. You can say, "I am starting to get out more and was wondering if you had any recommendations for good organizations and fun events?"

Next, we will discuss the next advanced strategy on how to work any room.

Keep Moving and Cover the Whole Room

Here's something that's key to remember when you are building social connections: your frequency of contact (i.e., the number of separate interactions) is much more important than having a long conversation with one or two people. When you go to events, you only need to talk to people for two or three minutes—five minutes max. Introduce them to someone else whenever you have the chance, and make sure to connect with the ones you see frequently.

Why the five-minute maximum rule? Here are a few reasons:

- You will meet more people and therefore practice your social skills. Social skills are learned behaviors, so the more you practice, the better you will get.
- You can worry less about what to talk about because you can ask a few quick questions and move on.
- You don't invest so much time in people that you end up missing out on other people in the room that may be better suited for you.

First, psych yourself up before you go to the event. Recite your story or affirmations as we discussed in chapter 4. You might also visualize that you are going to an event to meet old friends that you haven't seen in a while. This can relax you and your body so you seem more inviting to others.

Start working a room as soon as you arrive. I start before I even walk in the door. Talk to the valet and the doorman. These are great people for you to get to know. They know what's going on, they can help you out, and they're underappreciated. This also gets you warmed up and keeps your energy high. Otherwise, you can start to get self-conscious and nervous, and then social anxiety really kicks in. You'll start worrying about getting rejected and then feel all the negativity that people usually have in social situations. You will start overthinking what to do and relive your past negative social outcomes. Statistically, the longer you wait, the more unlikely you will be to engage others.

Start right away by asking the doorman what's up or tell him your name and ask him his name. Just say, "How's everything going?" Depending on where you are, you can greet the hostess or maître d' next. It's important to keep engaging people, even if you just say hi. You can stop and speak with them briefly or just say something and walk on by.

If you're at a charity, nonprofit, or networking event,

someone at the door will be checking people in. Stop and make sure your name's on the list and on their email list so you can get other invites. Ask how things are going. You can ask questions to learn quick tidbits about the organization and volunteer opportunities. I recommend you also do a little research prior to going to the event so you know who the organization serves, what their main functions are, and so forth.

Once you get into a room full of people, start making your way toward the bar, if there is one, or wherever it's natural for people to congregate, greeting everyone you pass as you go. Doing this keeps you in the moment and you don't have time for any social anxiety to crop up because you will be focused on talking to people.

From the check-in table to the bar, plan for brief, simple interactions—you don't have to worry about what to say. At this point you're not stopping to talk. You're just acknowledging and checking in with people as you cross paths with them.

Arriving at the bar is a good time to start a conversation. You can talk to the bartender or one of the people on either side of you. I always like to learn the bartender's name. Then when you come back, you can greet him and he will say your name back. People around you will think you are a VIP because he or she knows your name, and they will greet you like an old friend. Also, many bartenders and event staff eventually move on to other places, so you'll have connections in many bars, restaurants, and other places in your city.

The bar is also a comfortable place to start conversations because you have a real reason to be there. You are ordering a drink (or water) and waiting for the bartender. If there is no bar, just go wherever the food and beverages are.

So what do you say to people around you? We covered that before, but here are a few quick reminders. Go back to chapter 5 and review the material again on starting conversations.

- "How's everything?"
- "What do you have on the agenda this week/weekend?"
- "Are you a member of this organization?" If so, ask them about their favorite events or volunteer roles.
- "I'm really interested in attending some fun events and being a part of great organizations. Do you have any recommendations?" This question allows you get valuable information. Also, people like to be thought of as experts, and asking opinion questions are a good way to build initial rapport.
- Soon, you'll have the option to exchange information with them. Simply offer, "Let's exchange contact information and stay in touch about upcoming events." Or "I am gathering a list of events. Let's exchange information and I'll send them your way." Usually, I hand them my phone and they can put the information in faster and also their last name. More on exchanging information below.
- This process works because 99% of people talk rather than listen. You're going to stand out by asking questions about the other person first and taking a genuine interest. A great byproduct is that you leave the conversation with a little mystery around you— people are intrigued to learn more about you.

In a business context, make sure to focus on what you can do to help the other person. Since most people are concerned with their own personal gain, you'll quickly stand out. Start asking them questions about what they need, and you will quickly find out how you can help them. Albert Einstein once said, "Strive not to be a person of success, but a person of value." Start a conversation with something light and fun. Next you can ask, "What current challenges are you dealing with in your job (or company)?" Finally say, "How can I help you?" or "What can I do this minute to help you?" Then, write yourself a quick note about what is it, exchange contact information, and follow up within 24 hours. You might not be able to help them or provide them with a contact. Just tell them you tried—it will go a long way. I'd also come up with another potential way you could help them and see if that is of interest.

Introducing People to Each Other (Including Strangers)

Introducing people to other people *is by far the most powerful way to build social capital*. It doesn't matter where you are or if you know anyone. When you meet someone, ask their name, then turn to the person on the other side of you and introduce them. If they already know each other, they will tell you. If that's the case, you have a great conversation starter—how do they know each other? When you know people, introducing them to others makes you a great host, as it gives you the opportunity to make other people feel more comfortable.

But remember, if you don't know anybody, you can still introduce them. It's as straightforward as this: You are standing between two people and you turn to the one on your left and say, "Hi, how's everything going?" And then turn to the person on the other side, point at both of them, and say, "Hey, do you know each other?" If they don't, then you can reply, "Well, let me introduce you. I have no idea what your names are, but I'd like to introduce you to each other." Or "You two need to meet each other!" It's funny, but also genuine. And you can keep adding additional people to introduce to the original two people. Soon, you'll have created a group of people who've just met—who are all having fun getting to know each other and you haven't even moved. And you're the social hub who's made it all happen!

Friends and clients are always resisting doing this, and they come up with a ton of excuses. They say it seems really awkward, what if the people don't want to meet each other, how can this really work, etc. Well, I've introduced people to each other more than 100,000 times and I've never had anyone immediately turn away or say something rude or mean to me. The worst that can happen is that someone quickly disengages. That's only happened a handful of times. Most of the time, the people I've introduced are having a great time and a lively conversation, and many times they exchange contact information. People want to meet new people and they often don't meet anyone new when they are out. You are helping and serving them by providing an introduction to someone else. You never know what can come out of an interaction. I've been able to introduce people who have gotten married, run marathons together, become best friends or business partners, etc.

Let's try it out. I'm going to use the example of a man introducing a man and woman in the example here, but it works well no matter who's doing the introducing or being introduced:

- If both people hit it off and end up going out together, they will be grateful you introduced them.
- If they don't hit it off, the man will be grateful because very few men introduce a man to a woman and then walk away. Most men live in scarcity and they would look at every opportunity as scarce and try to hoard for themselves. But you see a world of possibilities and abundance, and giving as a part of who you are. So that man will admire you (on some level) and like you immediately. I call that almost instant rapport. And he then will introduce you to men and women he knows with enthusiasm and extend you some level of trust (i.e., social capital). That's a fantastic return on your time and effort.
- If they don't hit it off, the woman sees you as very confident and living a life of abundance with the opposite sex. You enjoy your life, help others, and enjoy being social. So if the woman approaches you or you run into her again, you have built instant

rapport and attraction with little to no effort. And she doesn't run across men like you often, so you have differentiated yourself as well. That's the beginning of a great opportunity for dating or building a friendship. And remember, this woman has friends she will enthusiastically introduce you to. That's creating abundance!

* And remember, this is equally powerful in a business environment.

Another great byproduct of this is that people are always introducing me to other people they know because I did the same for them. They don't normally do it, but they saw how easy it is and feel comfortable doing it around me. So that helps me meet even more people with little to no effort.

Finally, you don't need to keep the conversation going between the people you've introduced. Many times, I walk away right after I introduce them. They will keep the conversation going if they want to.

Now we will move onto another advanced strategy in this chapter on how to exchange contact information.

Exchanging Contact Information (Drum roll...)

Everyone wants to know how to ask for someone's contact information. It's really simple, so don't overcomplicate it, be confident and direct, and have a plan. That's why I also tell people to keep abreast of what's happening in your city: events, new restaurant or bar openings, art exhibits, charity or nonprofit or business networking events, etc. It's really boring for someone to say, "Let's get together sometime" or "Let's grab coffee." Everyone has heard that a million times. Be more creative and do something fun!

Here are several ways to do it:

"I enjoyed the conversation. There is a great charity event happening next week, we should check it out. Let's exchange information and go." Then hand the person your phone or offer to give them your information and have them follow up with you.

Maybe you both like running. You could say, "There is a great running club I belong to. You should come next Saturday and join us. Let's exchange information."

If you want to banter a bit, you can say, "It's been great getting to know you. We can't let this end right here. We need to stay in touch. Any ideas on how we can do that?" It's funny and original. If the person doesn't mention exchanging phone numbers, then you know you have some rapport building to do or it's time to walk away. Or you could say, "Let's get together soon. But we haven't exchanged phone numbers. Oh, that's right (and smile)." Finally, if you discussed something you like to do, you can say, "Well, now that we are doing XYZ activity, don't you need to ask me a question?" He or she may say, "What?" And you can say, "Really? Come on now! (and smile)." He or she will most likely say, "Exchange phone numbers?" and then you can say, "Wow, are you usually this bold asking for a phone number?" And then laugh or smile and take out your phone.

In a business setting, you will most often exchange business cards and follow up from there. So make sure you carry enough business cards and a pen so you can write down some notes on what you discussed, what challenges the person is facing, and how you can help them. If you run out of business cards, just get their card and follow up. If neither of you has cards, just exchange phone numbers or write down their contact information (phone number and email) and follow up. For all follow-up, you should do it in 24 hours or less to stay top of mind and to show them you valued the interaction enough to follow up immediately. You should also connect with them on their social media channels, such as LinkedIn afterward.

Let's cover the final advanced strategy in this chapter on how to meet and build relationships with key influencers.

Where to Meet VIPs in Your City

As we briefly discussed in the chapter on social capital, meeting influential people with large networks or the power to open doors can create limitless opportunities for you. You also will be perceived as powerful if you are seen spending time in their company, and if you can create meaningful friendships with them. When it comes to meeting VIPs or influencers, think big and go for it. The worst-case scenario is that nothing happens with them, but if somehow you can make it happen, it can be life changing. Pursue these people with good intentions, honesty, directness, and don't focus on their fame. Remember, these VIPs and influencers are people too, who have feelings, hopes, dreams, fears, insecurities, and goals. Help them achieve or advance something in their life they feel is meaningful and you can create a successful relationship.

Here some ideas to get you started:

Get to know local bloggers (or your favorite bloggers wherever they may be).

Every city has great food, fashion, nightlife, and charity blogs. Bloggers will give you information on new restaurant openings, fashion events, and other opportunities where you can meet some fantastic people in your city. I've also emailed questions and shared opinions with them to start off a relationship. Plus, you can meet the bloggers at events. If they get to know you, they may share with you media passes to major events. Remember, always try and be generous first, since bloggers get inundated with requests and meet a lot of people. Asking how you can help them first is an easy way to stand out. If a blogger isn't in your city, send an email stating what you like or admire about their blog and writings, state your value proposition and who you are, and provide some offer to help them. You also should comment and post on their blog posts on a regular basis. Don't miss out on this opportunity. I have some very good friends I have made this way!

Find the influencers in your city.

Every city has movers and shakers in the food, fashion, nightlife industries, and super networkers (i.e., people with several thousand connections). Find out who those people are in your town and visit their establishments. Introduce yourself if you can and think about how *you* could potentially add value to their business or endeavor. Perhaps you can throw a charity event to bring them some business and media attention. If your city publications have annual "Best of" lists, that's a great place to start, and you might even look to national honors like the James Beard Award for chefs. Look for lists such as the Top 40 Under 40 in your city or in national publications. Meeting people like this can help you build a powerful network, and you can also learn about organizations or events that you should check out and/or possibly the names of people who could open doors for you.

Finding super networkers is very helpful and can massively increase the rate at which you build social capital. How? Well, if you can establish a relationship with a person, they will introduce you to their network. By doing this, they are giving you trust and credibility with the people they interact with. That will help you meet them and build relationships with them. Never use this to be a social climber because it will eventually backfire, and karma has a way of coming back around. Remember to be generous with these people. Here is an example why: A good friend of mine, Jackson, lives here in Dallas. He is an extremely well networked person in the city (and beyond) and runs a very successful lifestyle management company. Jackson meets with a lot of people every week, and he always tries to help people in any way that he can. That's the common trait every super networker that "gets it" has—they lead with helping and giving with everyone. The challenge is most people that run across super networkers don't get it. They don't follow the fundamental principle of seeing every relationship like a bank. If you make more withdrawals than deposits, you'll have a negative balance, and that's a bad position to be in. People ask Jackson for things all the time (and I'm not referring to his clients), and they don't realize what it takes to make it happen. For example, if someone asks him to help them get into a restaurant with no reservations at the last minute, he can't just snap his fingers to make it happen. He has to make a phone call to get the restaurant to readjust other people and make it happen. Well, that's asking a lot of a restaurant so Jackson will usually owe them a favor or help down the line. If the person asking for help doesn't get what it takes to make a reservation happen and that they have to be willing to help in return, he can't keep helping that person. Plus, going out of your way for someone who constantly makes withdrawals gets old fast. So lead with giving and appreciate when someone like Jackson extends himself for you, and thank him directly. And if you do, he will know you get it and will be willing to help you significantly more down the line.

Today's employee is tomorrow's owner.
Everyone has to start somewhere. This is why it is important to get to know everyone you meet, from the bouncer to the hostess to the bartenders. Getting on a first-name basis with these folks now may pay off big-time down the road!

Create your dream list of people.
Write down 10-15 people on your target list of influencers in your city and beyond. Make sure you have specific reasons why you want to meet these people, what you admire or appreciate about them beyond just their fame or fortune, and how you can potentially help them. Create a plan for how to meet them whether it is in their hometown, at a conference, etc. You will need to get creative, assertive, and follow up as many times as necessary (and remember to befriend any gatekeepers to these people such as assistants, publicists, aides etc.).
So you have identified people you want to meet, what do you do next?

- You need to set up a meeting or find out where they are attending an event or conference.
    - Do your research and learn as much as you can about the person.
    - If you are writing an email, make it short and to the point. Tell them upfront why you are writing to them, and what you admire or appreciate about them. Offer something of value that you can do for them in the email. And finally, if you have friends in common, you could mention them as well, and especially if you have spoken to the mutual friends about that person and they recommended you reach out to them. Creating possible connections is always advantageous.
    - One of the worst things people do is ask a VIP if they can "pick their brain." Asking if you can pick the brain of someone who you don't know every well is clearly signaling you are only trying to extract value, rather than give it. You can stand out even further by offering something of value to a VIP, especially if it's something simple like a restaurant recommendation, a workout tip, vacation advice, movie suggestion, etc. The suggestion will be appreciated, and it will show you are considerate, you get the value of give-and-take, and you're not totally self-motivated. During your research on the person, you will get a better feel of what suggestions to offer based on what you learn. If you're at a loss for what to offer, here's a simple suggestion: Offer to do five days of charity work for their favorite charity in exchange for five minutes of their time. That's a win-win situation and something that will definitely stand out!
    - If you meet in person, be confident, focused, positive, and as though you belong there. Some

people act nervous, uncomfortable, fidgety, or talk way too much. You also can slow down your movements, including your smile. If you smile too quickly, it can come off as insincere, overeager, and/or star struck.

o   Rehearse the three things you want to say. This should include similar information as in your email, but be even shorter. "Hi XYZ, I'm ABC. It's fantastic to meet you." Pause and ask them a question about the event, conference, etc. Next say something about what you admire or find fascinating about the person and what they have done. Next, ask them what challenges they are facing. You may learn something valuable about how you could help them. Finally, offer something of value, why you want to connect, and suggest exchanging contact information and following up.

o   Sometimes you know you don't have much time to speak to someone. Perhaps you have only 30 seconds if other people are waiting, or you just know based on the environment you don't have time to interact with them, or you have a phone call with them and are not clear how much time you really have. In this case, you'll need to adjust your plan.

You could also use this process below to get a meeting or follow-up conversation. First, you need to convey credibility so they will continue to listen to what you have to say and move past any hesitations they have. Mention any mutual connections, your employer, something they would value based on your research, etc. You must establish some level of trust in the first 10-15 seconds. You don't need that much, but you do need a little. Use LinkedIn, Facebook, or other sites to find common or mutual contacts.

Second, state what your value proposition is and how it may be able to serve them. Make sure you do your research and figure out how you can potentially help the person.

Remember, you don't have much time, so it is all about them and what you can do for them. State that you want to find a way to better understand their current challenges and help them, and you are willing to do whatever it takes on their terms. It's not about selling yourself and sharing information about you. That's a recipe for the person to walk away or end the call. Third, suggest a meeting time to follow up, and then a compromise time such as whenever it is convenient with them. This shows you are willing to do whatever it takes to speak with them.

Finally, you may not have sold the person on the meeting and why they should take it. So you always want to have a fallback position that will leave them an opportunity to say yes. For example, you can let them know that even if they don't want to discuss XYZ, you'd love to get together based on your admiration for them and something specific they have done, praise from a mutual friend, etc. Remember to always create opportunities for people to engage you on their terms.

CHAPTER 7

THE KEYS TO SOCIAL LEADERSHIP

"Success comes from taking the initiative and following up . . . persisting . . . eloquently expressing the depth of your love. What simple action could you take today to produce a new momentum toward success in your life?"

—*Tony Robbins*

So You Have Their Contact Information. What Next?

I'm going to cover personal and social follow-up, then business separately. It is important to develop a system for following up, and you need to get in the habit of incorporating a giving philosophy in your interactions versus a *what can I get from them* mentality. Helping and inspiring are always more effective. You should also have a plan for contacting people regularly and creating deeper relationships over time. Finally, you have to lead by taking action. This chapter is about giving you the tools to be a leader in your life.

Following Up in Dating Situations

You get home from a great event and you want to follow up with someone you met. You are thinking, "Do I suggest a movie, dinner, drinks? What would be the best thing to do?" I would recommend a group activity. Invite the person to do something with your friends or in a group setting.

<u>There are several reasons for this</u>:

- When people interact 1:1, such as on a dinner date, it is much easier for someone to feel like they need to be on their best behavior. It's much harder for you to get a sense of their authentic self.

- In a group setting, you can see how they interact with other people and assess their social and communication skills, as well as get feedback from your friends on things you may miss. We all have our blind spots when meeting people, and your friends can help point out any red flags or provide positive feedback that cements what you were thinking. If you don't have any friends that can participate, you still can learn a lot regardless.

- In a group setting, they're going to be more likely to let their guard down. You get to see who they really are and if they're the type of person you want in your life.

- This also takes a lot of pressure off both people during the interaction, and that will help build rapport and a more positive overall interaction.

- It's much easier for a woman to invite a man to do a group activity, and it appears much less assertive.

- Group activities are fun and interesting, and it shows some interest and creativity to offer up a suggestion like this. It is much better than doing the typical drinks, coffee, dinner, brunch, etc. Plus, you allow the other person an opportunity to get to know what you like, who you are, and it lets you be a little vulnerable.

- Group activities can consist of a charity or nonprofit event, activity (interest group or sport), group of friends going out, etc. I'd avoid religious or political activities unless you know the other person shares your views.

When do you follow up? I would text or call the person the next day. There is no point in waiting, and playing games isn't good for any type of relationship—period. I don't think it matters whether you want to call or text, unless the other person has dropped a hint or said something that would indicate their preferred communication method. If you don't hear back, I'd contact them once more, and then if you don't hear back, move on. They may still get back with you, and could be busy at work or with other things going on. You never know what's going on in someone's life and it doesn't do you any good to assume, overanalyze, or stress out.

What do you say? I like to be direct, short, and to the point. Too many people carry on conversations over text instead of creating more urgency to meet and talk in person. You don't build relationships or rapport over text or on the phone. You do that in person. Use electronic communications to get online people offline. That's a huge key! In fact, the more you say, the higher the chance you may say something to negatively influence the outcome or turn someone off. Remember, you can't get the context from a text message.

You can say, "It was great to meet you on Saturday night at XYZ place. Are you free on Thursday? There is a great charity happy hour on Thursday for ABC organization at 7pm." Then sign your name, unless they already have it in their phone. Feel free to drop in some humor or banter as well, but don't have long conversations or ask a bunch of questions. Get to the point quickly, and save the questions for in person. You create an air of mystery, you don't seem too available or desperate, and you respect someone's time.

Whatever you do, DON'T text:

- Creepy one-liners such "hey baby…you wanna hook up?"
- Long, drawn-out questions such, "So where do you want to be in your life in five years?"
- Multiple messages if you don't hear back. This makes you appear very needy and as if you don't have anything else going on in your life.

- Two or three days later hoping to appear mysterious. It just comes off as though the interaction wasn't important or you're playing games.
- Agreeing with everything he or she says, especially with exclamation marks. It comes off as too excited and could be seen as desperate. Plus, this isn't the time for an extended conversation to begin with.
- Past 11pm. This screams "booty call." Unless you have established that is what your relationship is or that contact at that time or later is fine, text earlier.

Moving forward, I think it's a good idea to mix in 1:1 time with group activities. It goes a long way in any relationship to create memories and fun experiences that you can look back on over time. It also injects excitement and exploration into your interactions.

Also, I hear from lots of people who want to know how you can invite someone over to your place after you get their contact information. My advice? If you go this route, keep it casual and be patient. Just say, "I'm planning on watching a movie and having some wine on XYZ night. Feel free to join me." This way someone doesn't feel pressured or obligated to come over, and they can respond if they choose to. You could use a similar text or email to meet for drinks or an activity if they don't want to meet at your place. If you've had a really great time with someone you've just met, you can say something similar at the end of the night, but know that some people just aren't that comfortable going to the home of someone they don't know well.

I have a lot more information, opinions, and research on dating advice for both women and men on my website. I've heard almost every possible story, and could write a book on the funny and crazy things I've heard from clients, friends, and acquaintances. So check it out if you want more information.

Inviting New Acquaintances to Events or Group Activities

Now that you have contact information for people that you've met socially, what do you do to follow up with them? A fantastic way to stay connected and build relationships is to invite new acquaintances to events (charity, nonprofit, etc.) or activities you're already into—salsa dancing, rock climbing, or wine tasting, for example.

How? Here are two quick ways:

1. You can invite people to events on Facebook in a snap. If an event you frequent has a Facebook event page, go to it and click "Invite Friends." If you want to invite a lot people at once to a Facebook event, you can use Google Chrome and download an extension that will allow you to invite hundreds of people in seconds. What I have done is created groups on Facebook with my friend list, which separates the people into distinct buckets. I've made groups for people who like charity events, art events, etc. This way I can invite people to things that they may be interested in going to.

2. You can also invite people via text or email. Just make one email and copy/paste it. "Hope you are having a good week. Feel free to join me at a great event, XYZ, at X time on Y day. If you have any questions, let me know." I recommend inserting their first name in the text message, and not sending a mass text message. Make sure you send it to just one person. People typically don't appreciate being on mass text messages sent out to 10 or more people.

People are always looking for something fun and different to do, and they will appreciate your effort. Don't worry who or how many people show up; more and more people will over time. You will find that some people may not show up at anything for a long time, and then all of a sudden they'll be regulars.

The byproduct of reaching out is that people will now start sending you invites to events and private get-togethers such as dinner parties, birthday parties, New Year's parties, themed events, holiday parties, etc. You will get a whole new stream of invitations. Don't go overboard, though. You don't want to annoy people by sending them invites every single day. Stick to three to four times a month per person for invites.

Finally, I've found over the years that people appreciate the invite even if they never go. People come up to me all the time thanking me for taking the time to invite them to events, even if they haven't come to one in years. Keeping people in your thoughts and taking action is very powerful.

Getting Together in Groups: Champagne Thursday

Here's something I did twice a month for a long time, and it worked really well. On Sunday or Monday, I texted or emailed people to meet up at a centrally located hotspot in Dallas. I'd say something like, "Hope you are having a great week. Join us for Champagne Thursday at XYZ place at 7:30pm. Look forward to seeing you." Don't worry if people don't respond or if your network is small. Everyone has to start somewhere. Finally, you can get people together for any reason…it doesn't have to be meeting up for drinks. Be creative and have fun!

This kind of group get-together is great because:

- You are the social hub bringing people together.
- You're going to get to know new people better.
- You are a gracious host who will introduce strangers and get the party and fun started.
- You can introduce them to the bartenders, waitstaff, and others, even if you don't know them at all.
- You practice your social skills and taking a leadership position.

Doing this is free, easy, and makes you stand out from the crowd. People don't get to meet new people that often so you are helping them out, and it's an attractive opportunity for them.

Build Deeper Relationships in Your Social Life

Once you're on your way meeting a lot of people, how do you start building deeper relationships with them? How about arranging a small dinner party or brunch? It doesn't have to be elaborate, and aim to invite no more than six people. Just find a good place for dinner on a Wednesday or Thursday or brunch on Saturday or Sunday, somewhere centrally located, and text or email people four to five days in advance: "Hi (name of person), I hope you are having a fantastic week (or weekend). I'm getting some people together for (dinner or brunch) on X day at Y time. Are you free to join us?"

This is a great way to spend more time getting to know someone and find out if that person is someone you get along well with. You can organize these small gatherings once a week, and you can mix up the attendants. If you call and speak to the manager of the restaurant and tell them what you are doing, they'll often give you a special discount or offering, like free beverages or free appetizers or name cards for your group, especially if you bring regular business to their restaurant.

You can organize 1:1 interactions, but it is good to start to get to know people a little bit to make sure they are a good fit for you, and vice versa.

Lastly—and this is hard for some people—you are going to have to be vulnerable in your relationships and let people in. Part of moving relationships forward is getting to know someone. You can do that quicker by sharing personal information with others in the appropriate time and place. Tell someone a story from your childhood that was a meaningful, funny, or positive experience. Share some current challenges in your life, and open up on how they are affecting you. Discuss a subject or topic that you are really passionate about and why it matters to you. This allows others into your life and breaks down the walls between you, and allows for transparent communication. It also helps someone else feel comfortable to share important things in their life with you. By taking the lead and sharing first, you create an opportunity for the other person to be open. Some people have a hard time opening up, and see it as a risk to do so.

Great Ways to Enhance Your Relationship with Your Partner

We covered how to follow up with new acquaintances and people we may date. What about following up with your current intimate relationship? Romantic relationships are a very complex topic, and there is way too much ground to cover in this book. It's one of the most important areas in our lives, and I highly recommend investing time and energy in creating successful mindsets and habits here.

I do want to cover one activity you can do if you are having challenges with your partner or feel like you just are not connecting with them.

Step 1: Plan a dinner at a restaurant, or create a romantic setting at home (or away) with wine, candles, etc. You want to set the stage for a more intimate setting where you can freely share, communicate, be present and not distracted, and be emotionally invested. Think of what you want the outcome to be, and what you want to convey to your partner.

Step 2: Tell your partner two things that you really appreciate about them, and how they have positively impacted you. Be very specific. Don't just say, "I really appreciate you." Or "I really appreciate you for all the things you do." What are those things? Why are they important? What impact have they had? How did they make you feel? How would your life be if they hadn't done that? Put some skin in the game and lay it all out there so you can lead and show your vulnerability. This will set the tone for the rest of the night. If written communication is more your style, you can give them a card with a handwritten, heartfelt note as well.

Step 3: I believe if you ask better questions, you get better outcomes. So plan a few questions you can ask that allow your partner to truly express him or herself without feeling like they'll be judged or criticized.

Here are some questions or topics you can discuss:

- Recall an amazing experience or happy time you both experienced. When was it? What were you doing together and how did it make you feel? Could you plan a similar activity in the future?
- Is there an activity that you could start doing together that you both are interested in?
- Can you set up a regular time every week to connect 1:1?

Step 4: Remember to be an active listener in the conversation. When emotional topics arise, it is easier to want to talk more or try and think of things to say and not really listen to the other person. But listen. Be patient, open minded, genuine, and willing to take action. Don't make promises because you think that's what the other person wants to hear; you need to be yourself. Compromise is essential in life, but not at your own expense.

Step 5: Rephrase your conversation so the other person truly knows you listened and got it. You can always ask questions to clarify. Now, commit to the plan you discussed, and put it in action!

CHAPTER 8

SOCIAL WEALTH STRATEGIES FOR BUSINESS, DEALMAKING AND NETWORKING

"The currency of real networking is not greed, but generosity."

—Keith Ferrazzi

We've talked a lot of so far about business, dealmaking and networking, and creating your life plan and your personal brand. I hope this book has inspired you to set those in motion if you haven't already. This chapter is going to focus on additional ways you can create the relationships you need and build your social capital in the business world.

Rapid Relationship-Building

Your success is based in many ways on the people you know. You can't do it all alone. In the long-term, relationships are the number-one way to create the success you want. So it makes sense to meet the influencers that can help you the most, whether they are local or somewhere else in the world.

If you want to make your network work for you, you will need to invest substantially in your relationships, deliberately and consistently. As you'll see, lots of the tips we have discussed are useful in your personal life as well as your business life.

We've talked a lot about adopting a giving mentality to help others and advance your own career and goals at the same time. Thinking about what you can do for others creates social capital, builds trust, and sets you apart. Generosity builds strong relationships quickly. When you meet someone new it is always a potential business relationship. So always directly ask them about their current challenges in their career and/ business so you can see how you can be of service. Then ask yourself, "How can I be of value to this person?" Use that as the lead in every interaction you have. Give, give, and give in those interactions.

Be a Connector

Malcolm Gladwell, in his book *The Tipping Point*, writes about the power of connectors. Connectors bring together people and spread trends and extend information. Connectors show real power because they are indispensible to others. Other people see connectors as power brokers in information, and as a valuable resource when they are stuck or need to connect with someone.

Networking is a two-way street. While you should always be looking for people to mentor and guide you, it is just as important to find people you can help. If you hear of a job lead that would be perfect for one of your contacts, pass it on. If you meet someone you think would be a beneficial contact for your colleague, introduce them.

When you meet people, think of how you can help them and what resources you can offer them. It can be something small. You will be amazed at what will happen and how addicting it will be. You can start right now, and you don't need to know many people to begin.

Develop Your Networking Plan

Life doesn't just happen for you. You need to be purposeful. So it's time to create your networking plan and take action. If you want to meet the right people, you must be focused and clear on who they are, why you want to meet them, and how you can add value.

Don't know how to get started? Here is a process you can use.

Once you figure out your life plan, you'll have a stronger sense of who can best help you along your life path. Get organized about it. You can use a spreadsheet to list your contacts and chart your progress with them. Here's how:

Person & Company Names (Column 1): List 10–20 people who can help you advance your goals. Use Google to research individuals who would be able to offer guidance or function as mentors. These people can be anywhere, not just in your town. Unless you live in a small town, travel extensively for work, or have the means to travel and meet them, make sure about 50% of these contacts are local. Prioritize your list in order of what's most important to you. You can usually figure out someone's email, or at least their Twitter handle, by Googling them, or by exploring their company website. Send them a short note asking for the meeting and let them know that you'd like to help them with their ongoing project or mission (more on this below). See the section on meeting VIPs and influencers; you can use that contact process here too.

Outreach Plan (Column 2): What's your outreach plan for each person? Is it a phone call? Coffee? Drinks? Never ask for more than 30 minutes of someone's time. For phone calls, ask for no more than 15 minutes. It is much harder to turn down a modest time request than a big one.

Goal (Column 3): What's your goal? What do you want to get out of this interaction? Do you want a mentor? Do you want to sell something or partner with this person? Do you want to write a book with them?

Giving/Helping (Column 4): What can you do for the other person? Do your research, and you *will* find opportunities. Maybe someone is heavily involved in a charity organization. You could throw a small happy hour to raise money, get involved with the organization, or find sponsors for an upcoming event.

Talking Points (Column 5): Write down three to five main talking points so you have a clear plan of approach when you have your meeting.

Current Status (Column 6): Keep track of where you are with your outreach. Note if you've received a response or set a date to connect, or the outcome of your meeting.

Relationship Status (Column 7): Rate where you believe that relationship is on a scale of one to five (with one being weak and five being very strong).

Anything Else? (Column 8): Use this column for extra notes.

Review these metrics monthly to assess where you are and what the next steps are according to your list. You may realize you need to add or delete people from the list.

Finally, make sure you try to stay in contact through social media on an ongoing basis. If you can get their email, connect with them on LinkedIn. If they have a Twitter, Pinterest, or Instagram account, follow them, and comment on their tweets and add additional value such as links to other articles.

Where to Network for Business

We've discussed where to go to meet people. This applies for networking for business, finding potential clients or partners, funding your business, and more. It's more powerful and influential to network and find commonalities with people outside of a business context. People can get to know who you are and what you are about. That builds trust and credibility (see the social capital chapter for reference).

People also want to see your passion and excitement when you are doing something you really like or love to do. Connecting with others over your shared passions is a very powerful way to build initial rapport and connections. So sit down and make a list of the things you love to do, and then go out and do them. For example, I love to exercise so I participate in number of activities. I love to plan charity events and be involved with nonprofit organizations, so it is something that is easy to do because I am passionate about doing it, and it isn't a chore or something I have to psych myself up to do. Perhaps you love to cook, so join a cooking class or an organization that throws dinner parties. You can also combine things you love: running with charity. Leukemia & Lymphoma Society has a Team in Training event where you raise money by doing marathons, triathlons, cycling, etc. There are limitless things you can do, and that's exciting.

You can check out business networking events, your local Chamber of Commerce, or just Google *business networking* and your city. The challenge at some of these events is that some people are mainly looking for opportunities, rather than real connections.

Attending Conferences

Most experts agree that the top benefit of conference attendance is the value people get from networking and the relationships they build there. Where else can you find so many industry contacts facing the same issues as you or your organization? Are there solutions you're not aware of and "potholes" you can learn to avoid? You can also through networking create partnerships or sales when you are at a conference either directly with the people you meet or indirectly through their contacts.

Well, many people who attend conferences don't leverage the limitless gains you can make by meeting people because they don't have a strategy in place before they attend. You need to know the people attending, do your research, and set up meetings or seek out those people you want to meet. I want to share with you some ideas and strategies that can give you a leg up on everyone else and potentially create a life-changing situation for you when you attend:

- Put together a list of ten local and national events that would be strategic for you personally and for your company or business. Commit to going to at least two of them.

- In the first column of a spreadsheet, put together a target list of all the attendees and speakers that you want to meet. The next four columns contain why you want to meet them, three bulleted speaking points, what value can you deliver to them, and, if they are speakers, when they speak. Also, do research on each person and see if you can find out their passions, interests, charities they are involved in, industry challenges they may have, and people you have in common (use LinkedIn here).

  You can also share the list with your boss or manager, and see if there is anyone they want you to connect with. This way, you are being a strategist for the company, not just yourself.

  Then, carry this list with you at all times, so you can keep track of whom you have spoken with, and whom you haven't. After the conference, report back on the true return-on-investment, not only from potential deals, but the new relationships you've created that can help the company or your business move forward.

- Enlist several people from your company that are attending the conference, so you can coordinate and synchronize your lists to reach even more people. Plan times to walk around together and meet with people or tag team for dinners or lunches. Going offsite for meals can be great because there are fewer distractions, and less opportunity for someone to potentially hijack the meeting. Before the conference even starts, you can get the list of attendees and speakers, which helps you with the above strategies. Contact them ahead of time and try to coordinate meetings. This way you don't leave anything to chance. Next, instead of waiting in the long lines at the end of a speaker's speech, you want to try and speak with them *before* they go on stage. You will get more time with less effort, and you can wish them good luck. Then when you see them later, you can say, "It was great to connect before your speech…" and then mention something they discussed in their speech, that you'll be following up, etc.

- You can call or email the conference organizer and offer to help. Putting a conference on is tough in today's environment. If you offer to help, you may get free passes to events and invites to VIP receptions. Plus, you immediately stand out for offering to help. But this isn't giving to get something, so you have to be prepared to help and not get anything in return.

- Having a powerful mindset can get you past social anxiety or fears you have when approaching people. I highly recommend doing affirmations a week before the conference. What do you do? Write no more than three sentences in the present tense about how you'll succeed at the conference, have massive success, and blow by all your goals. Obviously, make sure you have clear goals and outcomes before doing this. Here's an example:

I am going to be a **MASSIVE SUCCESS** at XYZ conference!

1. Approaching people at the conference is easy. Everyone I meet loves speaking with me. I am

always able to help them, and they can help me achieve my goals.

2. People are excited and passionate about continuing our conversation and they want to introduce me to other influencers because they know I am an invaluable resource.

3. Etc.

Make sure you keep your affirmations in the present tense because it will help keep you in the mindset that it is happening now, and that's invaluable when you are actually at the conference. If you do it in the future tense, then what you want to happen will always be in the future. Don't use negative words like can't, won't, shouldn't, either. Reword the sentences with positive, action-oriented words that get you excited and your blood flowing.

Also, you need to get physically excited before you recite your affirmation to be in a mental state for peak performance. Do some form of vigorous exercise like jumping up and down, running, speed-walking, etc. This will get you focused in the moment and fully immersed in the current activity—your affirmations.

Next, visualize yourself at the conference and see yourself being successful there. See all the details, and hear the sounds. Think of this like watching a movie reel. It is important to say your affirmation out loud and hear yourself. Finally, you want to do this twice daily for one week prior to the conference, the morning of each day of the conference, and at any time during the day you need to get psyched up. If you're at the conference, you probably won't be able to get physically excited or recite it out loud, but that's ok.

I have tested the above process on thousands of people and it works very effectively. It's a strategy that will help propel you past fears, doubts, and uncertainty.

Once it works for you, it will continue to work, propelling you even further.

Here are additional things to keep top of mind when you are at conferences:

- Remember to review conversation starters to establish rapport and gain credibility. You can mention that you read that they are interested in XYZ or that you have a mutual acquaintance.
- Consider your body language—nonverbal communication is critical.
- In your conversations, you want to move quickly through small talk into the heart of the matter: challenges the person is having and how can you help them (including introducing them to other people at the conference...always be thinking of connecting others). You also want to succinctly state your greatest need.
- One key strategy here is listening versus talking too much. This will make follow up much more effective, and your chances of setting up future meetings are greatly enhanced. Then, after you get through this information, move on quickly. You don't have time to waste just chatting. Be strategic in your communications and time, and also remember you need to make a real, human connection here.
- Write down any notes on business cards when you exchange them so you don't forget key points, otherwise you'll be overwhelmed trying to remember everything that happened and will likely forget something important.
- Influential people attract other influencers...think bees to honey! So interact with the people around influencers and you will meet some fantastic new contacts.

- After the conference, immediately follow up with everyone, follow through on what you said you could do for them (or tell them you are working on it), and set up future meetings. Be persistent in follow-up if necessary; don't miss out on an opportunity. If you need to go through a gatekeeper, such as an assistant, be positive and excited when you speak to them. They are a potential ally and can help or hinder you getting on the person's schedule. Sometimes, I've had to call back many times to get a meeting, and have sent assistants flowers and books to thank them for their time. Do whatever it takes and be creative (and thoughtful). Also, reflect on the conference and your goals there, and consider what you did well and what you could do better the next time.

- Finally, consider speaking yourself. There limitless ways on a local or national level to become a speaker. You can use Google to help you find conferences that would be of interest of you. You should contact the conference organizer ahead of time, and start building a relationship with him or her. Ask what topics they are looking for speakers on.

  Next, identify what you want to speak about. We discussed building your brand before, and you want to stay consistent with that. You will need to develop an abstract that includes your topic, why it is compelling to the audience, and the three to five main takeaways attendees will get from your speech. Focus on major challenges people in your industry are having. Do research, speak to colleagues in your business and even competitors, maybe even do your own small survey. Then develop your presentation. Use imagery and minimal text on your slides with five to seven words per bullet maximum. You can find people to help you build images on slides pretty inexpensively with websites such as Fiverr.com. Conference organizers prefer high-visibility presentations. Finally, learn to speak effectively or become a better speaker by attending a local chapter of Toastmasters.

How to Follow Up in Business or Networking Situations

Once you've gotten someone's business card, how do you follow up with them? Most people never follow up, and that's what will give you a major advantage over them in the business world.

- When someone hands you their business card, write some helpful notes about them on it if it's appropriate to do so. Beware: In some cultures (such as in Japan) it is highly offensive to do this kind of thing.
- At the end of the night, spend a couple of minutes sorting through the business cards you've collected according to your priorities and categories.
- Rank the importance of each business card by how they fit into your network and how you can help each other.
- Follow up with a personal email or phone call within a couple of days.
- Make sure you add them to your LinkedIn network. If you are not on LinkedIn, join today. It's a great way to connect.
- Invite them to a future event that you are attending or keep them in the loop about an event you know they may be interested in.

What do you say in your follow-up? Thank them for their time, briefly remind them who you are and your value proposition, restate the main details from your conversation, and update them on any action items you discussed. You can also ask them if there is anything you can do to help them. You will want to suggest a time to meet with them at the close, and an alternative option as well. Don't be afraid to email someone immediately after you meet them. You don't have to wait.

Don't worry if they don't follow up. People get busy, and in most cases it has nothing to do with you. Contact their office or their assistant, and do whatever it takes to get the meeting. Be persistent and creative. It may take months or longer with some people. If you don't get the meeting, the next time you see them at an event, just be cordial and gracious—and the great conversationalist you're learning to be!

Stay in Touch

The most important part of building and maintaining a professional network is staying in touch. Sending quick, casual greetings on a regular basis will keep the connection alive so the next time you see someone, you won't be met with a blank stare. In order to maintain secondary relationships, I recommend getting in touch on a quarterly basis. You could do anything from tweeting to congratulate them on some company success or milestone to dropping them an email wishing them a happy holiday (if one is upcoming), being sure to include information that may be helpful for them or that they would find interesting (maybe information on a competitor, a new restaurant in their city, etc.), and mention that if there is any way you can be of service to let you know.

Finally, remember their birthday (if you know it), and instead of posting online alone, send them a handwritten birthday card. Send cards around the holidays, too. No one does this anymore, so you'll stand out from everyone else. You can also try a service like one from bondgifts.com that will send a handwritten note on your behalf.

Mentors

People who truly want to master their life have mentors to teach them the quickest path to success in all areas of their lives. You don't need to reinvent the wheel or spend a lot of time figuring something out that someone else has already mastered. They have done all the trial and error already for you, and they know the shortcuts. You will spend 10 times as long and a lot more money trying to do it yourself.

Think about it how we have passed along information over the history of the world. Most people learned by working as apprentices to people who had mastered their chosen field. But today, people have no patience—they want everything now. Many people refuse to commit, and instead eventually fail or give up because they don't understand the full process of change and the power of the mind, body and spirit. If you want to get extraordinary results, you have find people that can help you "win" in life.

CHAPTER 9

OPTIMIZING SOCIAL WEALTH: FINE-TUNING TIPS

"Friendship is horizon - Which expands whenever we approach it."

—*E.R. Harlip*

Now that you're well on your way to social mastery, here are a few extra tips to help you fine-tune your new social life.

Stay Present and Pay Attention

Whether it's in a business setting or on a date, the number-one way you can turn people off in your initial conversation is by not being present. Many people look around the room or don't have or keep consistent eye contact. Looking around, taking a phone call, or glancing at a text says you have something better to do, and that your current conversation is not that important to you. Put your phone away, look your companion in the eye, and focus, even if you're having just a 30-second conversation. People need to know you value your interaction.

Dress Your Best

Most people feel more confident when they're well dressed. This doesn't mean dressing expensively or wearing something uncomfortable, like a tight belt or high heels. What it means is taking pride in your appearance and showing up as your best self to social and business situations.

Women's fashion changes so rapidly, it's important to take a look at blogs and get a feel for what is in. You can find similar pieces much more affordably.

Here are a few blogs to check out that will give you plenty ideas of fashion for all different types of work environments and affordably priced options:

corporatefashionista.com
pinkpeonies.com
saucyglossie.com
thistimetomorrow-krystal.blogspot.com
vivafashionblog.com
wherewearinthecity.com

A few quick tips for men:

- Wear clothes that complement each other. I prefer solid shirts. Stripes and designs can accent the wrong things and take people's eyes off of you and onto what you are wearing—in a negative way.
- Take good care of your clothes. That means they need to be clean, for starters, with no wrinkles, holes, or stains. If you're going to an event, press your shirt ahead of time and polish your shoes or boots. Check out Kirby Allison's Hanger Project (hangerproject.com) for a wide range of ways to care for your clothes and shoes. For example, getting the right hangers for your clothes makes a huge difference in maintaining their shape and longevity. Don't skimp.
- Before a big event, get a haircut or trim, and make sure you are well groomed.
- Add a bit of cologne or fragrance if you like, but keep it light in business settings. In personal and social situations, you have more latitude. Check out these fragrance reviewers on YouTube to get the latest information on designer and niche fragrances at all

price points: Redolessence, mrzayas81, dracdoc, NY Goodsmellas, and ManLovesCologne

- Skincare matters a lot, so make sure you have a routine. Check out magazines or blogs to learn about the latest items on the market. A YouTube reviewer that has some great tips for every budget is Maximilian Heusler. You should check him out. Here are a few other options: groominglounge.com, manface.co.uk (look under skin care), and www.scform.com.

- I like wearing dark jeans and a blazer in casual social situations. Get a good suit for business and more formal outings, along with a tuxedo (as you grow your wardrobe). You can find inexpensive options out there, but don't get poor quality fabrics. Being well dressed creates more attraction as long as you carry if off with confidence. Antonio Centeno, www.realmenrealstyle.com, has great fashion and style tips, along with custom-made suits, and affordable alternatives. Here are a couple more blogs you can check out: dappered.com, effortlessgent.com, mensstylepro.com, and stylegirlfriend.com.

- Add a pocket square if you wear a jacket. Women love it and it gives them a conversation starter. It is unique, as most guys don't wear one.

One more thing: Exercise and nutrition really matter, along with eating well. Invest in this area. One of my clients, Ted Ryce, has a ton of great information for both women and men on his website, alphamanproject.com. Check it out. Alternatively, there are a ton of great group exercise options. I go to a place called Tread Fitness in Dallas. At places like Dallas's City Surf Fitness, you can incorporate surfing into your fitness routine. Fitness boot camps are very popular too. Finally, if you really want to take it to the next level, you can train like a Navy SEAL at extremesealexperience.com!

Throwing Events and Parties

Planning events is a fantastic way to meet people; open up many opportunities in your city; build connections with bars, clubs, and restaurant managers; and create valuable business connections. It is actually pretty easy to plan and hold an event; it doesn't have to take that long to put together and you can pull it off at little or no cost to yourself.

Here's what you need to do to create a successful event with only a few hours of work:

1. **Pick a date,** preferably four weeks in advance on a Thursday. You will get the highest turnout on this day, and four weeks gives you time to plan and promote. I like 7–10pm (or 6–9pm) to hold events because it gives people enough time to get to your event and be there for a while.

2. **Pick a central location** in your city and look for a couple of upscale bars or restaurant settings. Tools like Yelp, Urbanspoon, Chowhound, and Trip Advisor are great for this. Or search online magazines such as CultureMap or UrbanDaddy.

3. **Pick a local charity** or nonprofit organization to involve and raise money for. Why? First, you are helping a worthwhile cause. Second, your attendance will be higher because people like to help. If you can find an organization with a young professionals' group that could attend and help promote your event, all the better.

4. **Contact the charity** or nonprofit organizations and see if they are interested in participating. Tell them you are charging $10 at the door, and all the proceeds will go to them. If they say yes, then ask them to help promote the event on their social media channels, website, and through their email list. Ask if they're willing to lend a couple of people to come to the event to help with check-in and collect the money.

5. **Contact the bar or restaurant,** and ask to speak to the manager. Tell them about your event and the charity or nonprofit organization involved. Ask the manager for drink specials. I like asking for wine, champagne, and vodka specials. Then the bar can make money off other drinks, so it is a win-win situation. Ask to reserve a special area for your group. If possible, it's better to meet the manager in person to discuss these details.

6. **Contact photographers** and see if someone will photograph the event for free because it's for charity. In return, you can promote the photographer on social media and at the event.

7. **Create a Facebook event,** and invite people in your city. You can add the young professionals' group as a co-host/admin and the restaurant or bar as well, and they can invite their lists. So you really don't need to have much of a list yourself. You can also promote the event to bloggers in your city.

8. When you go out, **mention your event** to people you run into and send them the event invite.

9. You could **add a theme and a DJ**, but it is not necessary.

10. On the day of the event, **get to the location an hour ahead of time** to do setup.

11. **Put out a sign-up sheet** asking people to get on your email list in order to get updates about other parties.

12. **Greet people** as they walk in and welcome them to your event. If there are people at your venue who aren't a part of the event, greet them too. You may persuade them to join your event!

13. **Remember to introduce people to other people.** That can take your event from good to great.

That's it! Did you have fun? You got to meet a lot of new people, you are affiliated with a new charity or nonprofit organization, and you made a valuable new connection with a bar or restaurant manager.

Get Creative!

When I first moved to Dallas, I went out for brunch one Sunday—alone. I didn't know anyone yet, but I really wanted to make new friends. The drink special at the restaurant was dollar mimosas. I said, "I'll take ten." *Champagne for a dollar?* I thought. *I'm going to order ten and pass them out to some new friends.* When the drinks were all lined up, I handed out mimosas to anyone nearby.

I had a great time, and people really appreciated the gesture. Within a few minutes, people were making toasts and having fun. I kept the mimosas coming. Within five or ten minutes, I'd met about 20 new people. Most people don't meet 20 new people in months, and I'd done it in the course of one brunch. So when you come across similar opportunities, take advantage of them. It's a great way to stand out and make new connections easily. Something like I did is simple, cost-effective, and anyone can do it. It's not about the alcohol or giving away things for free, it is about being creative and meeting new people.

CHAPTER 10

IT'S GO TIME!

"Connection is the energy that is created between people when they feel seen, heard, and valued—when they can give and receive without judgment."

—*Brene Brown*

Feeling great about going out and meeting new people? You should be. You're ready. You don't have to wait for the perfect moment because that moment is NOW. You can get out there *tonight* and start expanding your network, building your social capital, making friends you'll have for life, finding romantic partners, and creating life-changing business opportunities. Your life is comprised of relationships. Invest in them.

As I've been saying throughout the book, you need to commit and do it now. The law of diminishing intent, popularized by self-help guru Jim Rohn, says if we don't take immediate action when we come across or uncover new ideas when our emotional state is high, the urgency starts to diminish rapidly. Soon, the goal of learning something isn't top of mind anymore and we never act. The key is to not only to want to learn, but to act as you learn. If you get ready for a big presentation, but never give it, it was a huge exercise in futility.

Create the habit of taking immediate action today. Start with something small in this book, and do it right now. Not five minutes from now—immediately. You will have created a small victory, started to fuel your progress and begun to create more passion in your life. It will inspire you to take the next small step, and the next small step, and so on.

Your life is a series of small, daily victories that culminates in major life transformation and changes that actually stick over time. What's also truly fantastic here is small changes affect everything else in your life, including the people in it. Nothing is compartmentalized.

For example, creating better relationships in business will foster new skills in your personal life and create better friendships and romantic relationships. If you start to exercise three to four days a week, you'll be inspired to eat healthier, which leads to having more energy, which leads to you having more time to be active with your family and friends, which leads to learning new skills and interests, which leads to starting a new business, and so on. One small step can cause a major chain reaction that can lead to creating everything you want!

Start replacing scarcity, doubt, fear, and emptiness with abundance, confidence, certainty, focus, happiness, love, fulfillment, progress, and a feeling of being truly alive on your terms. Remember, this is *your* extraordinary life, not anyone else's!

Don't use the excuse that you can't do it or that you only can do so much. That just isn't true. You've just trained and conditioned yourself to accept less, and created the habits that go along with it. For example, if I asked you to run as fast as you and as far as you could, perhaps you could run a couple blocks. You'd then stop and say that's all you could do. Well, really...is it? Are you positive? What if I said rest for a couple minutes. Could you run a little more? What if, after you ran a little more, I said rest again? The point of this example is to show you that you have a much greater capacity for action and accomplishment than you really know. Your mind gives out because of your psychology and habits. The reality is you barely tap into your full potential at any time in your life.

Next, successful people realize there is no success without failure. When you prevent failure, you prevent success. Positivity and negativity need each other to exist in the world. You must embrace both and break down the walls between them. That means you must master not only success but failure and negativity. Be a master of procrastination so you can move beyond it every time it rears its ugly head. You are going to have to do battle with your demons to create the life you truly want. Remember to welcome all experiences in your life because you never know which one will turn it all around.

Finally, as I've seen with thousands of clients and tens of thousands people I have interacted with, making true progress typically stems from powerful moments in life. Hitting rock bottom and feeling like you are at the lowest point in life, when desperation is at a high, is one such moment. You've come down so low that you finally have had enough. You have no fear of losing anything because you don't feel like you have anything to lose. You are in a position of transformation and change because you are willing to do anything and everything to move forward. You are clear, focused, and certain the path from here must be up. Because you're already out of your comfort zone, your current habits, actions, and plans are open to complete change. Amid a massive crisis, there is a limitless opportunity before you and you are in a powerful state if you take action. People who have struggled with addiction, severe physical and mental illnesses, and financial troubles may know this feeling well.

You don't need to wait until you hit rock bottom to make change. But you do need to be at a point where what you want in your life is much more compelling than what you have. For example, let's say you are overweight now, and you are sick of lacking energy and feeling lethargic, and missing out on opportunities with your family and friends. You can create change if you have very compelling reasons that inspire and focus you. With them, you will be able to overcome procrastination, lack of motivation, doubt, fear, etc., because you will want this new physical body so badly you will do whatever it takes to get there! Nothing will stop you from moving forward and taking the necessary steps.

Your life changes in instant, the moment you commit

with certainty and resolve to go after the life you really want to have. Join me on this journey, and let me serve you as you create extraordinary relationships and your extraordinary life. If you can't tell already, I'm very passionate about people and change, and it's what motivates me and gets me out of bed every morning! I'm very excited for you, and I can't wait to hear your success story.

If you have questions or want to share your story, please contact me at beextraordinary.tv or email me at jason@ jasontreu.com

To recap what we've covered:

- Relationships are crucial to success in every area of our lives. Whatever we want to do in life is dependent on the relationships we have and create.

- Your success is directly correlated to making other people successful.

- Social capital is the way to meet people and build relationships to create limitless opportunities in your life. Spend time developing it, and you'll see the rewards quickly.

- You can start a conversation *anywhere*—the grocery store, Starbucks, the dry cleaners, the train station. Social and communications skills are learned behaviors so practice daily; it is the only way you can get better.

- "How's everything?" is the only phrase you need. That simple question opens all kinds of doors and you can use it anywhere.

- Put giving, helping, and inspiring first. It will make you stand out in any setting, and it's the easiest and most gratifying way to build your social capital. Life isn't a scorecard, so don't treat other people like it.

- Be authentic, vulnerable, honest, direct, and transparent in your communications with others to speed up the relationship-building process significantly.

- Be a social hub who connects others. Introduce everyone you talk with to somebody else. It's one of the most powerful and influential social skills you can cultivate and a great way to set yourself apart.
- You are one interaction away from having what you want in your life, so talk to *everybody* and *give* whenever you can.
- Your psychology and behaviors play a big role in the success or failure of your initial interactions and your ability to build successful relationships. Creating your life plan is critical to your success. Not having one is like a leaf blowing aimlessly in the wind. Get clear, focused, certain, and take immediate action. Finally, take time to create your personal brand and use it in every interaction you have.
- Some places are better than others for meeting people, such as charity, nonprofit, and cultural events, interest groups, etc. You can meet many more people here than in other settings. It is also a powerful way to network for business.
- Find a way to meet influencers and VIPs to accelerate success in every area of your life.
- Before you arrive at a business or social event or outing, recite your affirmations to get focused, positive, confident, and energetic. Start talking to people as soon as you arrive. Greeting the doorman, valet, or bartender is a great place to start.
- Keep the conversation light. Don't talk work, politics, or religion, and don't ask, "What do you do?" Ask for opinions on local restaurants, music, etc.
- In business or networking situations, find out what challenges someone is facing in his or her business. Next, focus on offering help. Whatever you need comes last.
- In business, create your people plan and execute it. Plan the plan, and then work the plan. Do a similar exercise when attending business conferences.

- Nonverbal communication is how you make your first impression, so focus on gaining mastery of the basic skills. Pay attention when you talk to someone. Make eye contact and don't fiddle with your phone or look around the room.
- Make sure you have a plan to follow up with people right away, stay in contact with them, and create deeper relationships over time for both your personal and business lives.
- Be direct, honest, and transparent in your interactions with potential friends or romantic partners, and have fun.
- Finally, find mentors and/or coaches to speed up your learning and mastery process by decades, and help get you where you want to be.

Remember the top reasons people go out:

1. To escape their boring lives
2. To meet people and be social
3. To meet someone of the opposite sex
4. To meet someone to advance a business need or career opportunity

Conversation quick-starters:

- "How's everything?"
- "What are you most excited about in your life right now?"
- "What projects are you working on that you are most passionate about?"
- "What do you have on the agenda this week/weekend?"
- "Are you a member of this organization?"
- "I'm really interested in attending some fun events and being a part of great organizations. Do you have any recommendations?"
- "Do you know any great restaurants nearby?"

But remember, it is more about delivery than content, so don't get bogged down trying to say something perfect. When the situation calls for it, use banter in your conversations and have fun.

We've covered a lot of material together in this book, and you now have all the tools you need to meet thousands of people in the next year and take your life to the next level. Whether you've just moved to a new city, you're getting out of a rut, you're looking for the perfect partner, or you're developing a terrific business network, you're ready. Now, it's up to you to take the next steps and make it happen!

> "In life you'll realize there is a purpose for everyone you meet. Some will test you, some will use you, and some will teach you. But most importantly, some will bring out the best in you."
>
> —Marc and Angel Chernoff

ACKNOWLEDGMENTS

I didn't end up where I am right now by myself. No man is ever an island. I'm truly grateful for every person I have met in my life. I would not be here today if it were not for so many people who have been gracious in their time, patience, help, love, friendship, forgiveness, and the many precious lessons I have learned from them. I also want to thank the thousands of people that I have come in contact with in coaching. I thank you for your time, pain you have openly shared, dedication to creating an extraordinary life, generosity, and willingness to take that leap of faith.

This book is the culmination of compassion, forgiveness, friendship, amazing relationships, love, tears, doubt, fear, uncertainty, faith, patience, kindness, giving, perseverance, commitment, growth, change, moments of almost giving up, champagne and wine drinking, and more.

There are so many people to thank, so here's a start: Aaron Steinmetz, Adrianna Butcher, AJ Tucker, AJ and Erica Sander, Alexandra Sardarian, Alison Wille Harris, Allison Edwards, Allison Holmes, Allison Johnston, Allison McCutcheon, Alison Volk, Amber Cradduck, Amy Donovan, Andrew Ballenger, Ann Heidger, Anthony Porcaro, Antwane Owens, Ariba Kamal, Arielle Mandell, Ash Ashutosh, Ashlee Vicars, Ashley Forrest, Ashley Mahon, Avi Adri, Barbara Tate, Ben Goodall, Binay Curtis, Blynn Austin, Bob Moats, Bob Wilson, Bobby Majumder, Bradley Wilson, Brandon Coxton, Brian Chaka, Brian Rolfe, Brian and Chrissy Rudman, Brian Wendel, Brocka Nolen, Brittney Peters, Brooke Burnett, Brayson and Bryn Burchfiel, Bukekile Dube, Calvin Zito, Cameron Goldade, Carla

Gourley, Caroline Lee, Carolyn Caple, Cat Mundy, Chandler Bolt, Chelsea Lish, Cheyenne Dazey, Charles Korrell, Chris Connar, Chris Jones, Chris Scheliss, Chris Selland, Chris Short, Chris Weyers, Christie Dames, Christie Douglass, Cindi Johnson, Cindie Kile, Claire Kahn, Claire Morgan, Clarissa Cardenas, Claude Ramos, Cori Reichenecker, Cory Grimes, Court Alley, Courtney Edwards, Courtney Marsh, Craig Phillips, Cynthia Smoot, Dale Anderson, Dan Pritchett, Dani DiPirro, Daren Martin, Darren Squires, Darren Rhyne, David Brown, David Groshoff, David Gutierrez, David Kiger, David Krane, David Libby, David Meehan, Dean Somes, Dean Simonek, Dee Anna McPherson, Denise M Walraed Dilan Prema, Don Jarred, Duane Badenhorst, Dwayne Hawkins, Eddie Hinojoza, Elizabeth Bautista, Ellen Flowers, Ellie Miles Couch, Emily Neumann, Eric Berwin, Eric Colton, Eric Lyons, Erica Diamond, Erica Yarbrough, Erin Boor, Evan Fritschi, Federico Perez, Gary deCastro, Gay Donnell, George Hunter, Giselle Phelps, GP Theriot, Grayson Wafford, Greg Gianforte, Greg Mykytyn, Haley Chappell, Haley Dugas, Halle Smith, Hamilton Sneed, Harry Pforzheimer, Hilary Kinzler, Hunter Howard, Hunter Sullivan, Hunter Woodlee, Jack Keller, Jackie Kim, Jacqueline McAllister, Jalin Wood, James Andrew, James Roper, Jamey Peters, Jamie Bloom, Jamie Novak, Jamie Singer, Jay Fishel, Jay Fultz, Jay Sternberg, Jay Ward, Jayne Scuncio, Jeffery Peterson, Jennifer Adair, Jennifer Baker, Jennifer McCrummen, Jennifer Styers, Jenny Conway, Jenny Goodson, Jeremiah Jude Miranda, Jeremy McKane, Jill Brandt, Jill Walter, Joe Rodriquez, Joe Vitu, John Armstrong, Johnny Jet, Jon Brown, Jon Cronin, Jon Morgan, Jenna and Jonathan Apgar, Judy Johnson, Julia Glenister, Julie Biber, Kara Yi, Karl Chiao, Kaitlan Moczulski, Katie Todd, Kathy Samoun, Keith Diamond, Keith Norton, Kelly McKeon, Ken Painter, Kent Arnold, Kerry Carmack, Kevin Hoque, Kert Platner, Kim Brown, Kim Dierks, Kim Fischer, Kippy Thomas, Kirby Allison, Kirby Hall Jackson III, Kirby Wilkerson, Kortney Oliver, Kristen Weber, Kristi Heinrich, Kristy Montoya,

Lacey Muckleroy, Landon Ledford, Laura Borgstede, Laura Noble, Laura Reeder, Lauren Ives, Lauren Pulido, Lauren Reise, Lee Haspel, LeAnn Cullum, Leslie Wood, Liani Kotcher, Lindsay Olson, Lindsey Lockhart, Lindsey Thomas, Lisa Bhattacharya, Lisa Strapp, Liz Le, Liz Striegel, Luis Sanchez de la Vega, Mara Gvozdenovic, Margen Gadd, Mark Heintz, Mark Miller, Mark Pirtle, Mary Elizabeth Russell, Mary Lynn Coyle, Mary Wardley, Matt Hatchell, Matt Kerr, Matt Martin, Max Borges, Meagan McCracken, Melanie McKay, Melanie Ofenloch, Meredith Miller, Micah Baker, Michael Holmes, Michael Martensen, Michael Salimbene, Michael Thacker, Michael Vernone, Michelle Pitoniak, Natalie Solis, Natalie Westbrook, Nathan Hanks, Nick Frank, Nick Thompson, Nikki Kerth, Noah Coleman, Niji Vohra, OJ DeSouza, Pat Parsi, Paul Miller, Paul Sartin, Peter Fan, Phil Dade, Rachel Watkins, Randal Davis, Rebecca Connar, Rebecca Stevens Crownover, Reed Byrum, Renee Loy, Rex Bush, Rhiannon Lee, Ricki Kim, Robert Harris, Roger Maese, Rosalyn Putnam, Ross Harris, Rusty Stone, Ryan Donovan, Ryan Sadkin, Sam Khoury, Samuel Liu, Sandy England, Sanj Mohip, Sara Wilkins, Sarah Obaidat, Scott Poulter, Sean Gilligan, Shane Dolgin, Shantal Howell, Stefan Wolf, Stephanie Livingston, Stephanie Sanchez, Stephen Hehn, Steve Benckenstein, Steve Donnelly, Steve Holton, Tamara Ireland Stone, Tammie Margolese, Thomas Stilling, Tiffany Vega Heath, Tim Smith, Todd Stevens, Tom Moroch, Tommy DeAlano, Trevor Rubel, Tyler Wagner, Valentina Burton, Venessa Yanez, Veronica Roper, Vodi Cook, Whitney Brune, and multitudes of mentors…and thousands more…and of course, my mom and family!

My little girl, Glenda, the first dog I adopted at the SPCA in San Francisco who lives in my thoughts daily and is happily running around in doggie heaven.

My crazy Jack Russell Terrier, Napoleon, who was the best writing partner I could ever ask for. He drives me up a wall (daily), makes me laugh, gives me strength to move forward when I don't think I can, and licks my tears away.

I'd like to thank my awesome editor, Lindsey Alexander, for all her help, guidance, and support, and doing it whatever it took to help me. Finally, I'd like to thank Rick Duris, my copywriter extraordinaire...sales funnel guru...and...more. I deeply appreciate your time, energy, belief, help and making me laugh during some very challenging times.

ABOUT THE AUTHOR

Jason Treu is a top business and executive coach.

Jason simplifies business problems and guides business leaders to previously unimagined accomplishments. He helps them find the shortest, simplest path to exponential success and to become visionary leaders. That's why his clients across the world call him the "CEO's Secret Weapon."

Jason also has "in the trenches experience" helping build a billion-dollar company and working with many Fortune 1000 companies. He's worked alongside well-known CEOs such as Steve Jobs, Mark Hurd (at HP), Mark Cuban, and many others.

Through his coaching, his clients have met industry titans such as Tim Cook, Bill Gates, Richard Branson, Peter Diamandis, Chris Anderson (Owner of the TED conference), high profile VCs and investment bankers, and many others. He's also helped his clients create more than $1 billion dollars in wealth over the past three years and secure seats on influential boards such as TED and xPrize.

Jason has published three books. His bestselling book, Social Wealth, the how-to-guide on building extraordinary business relationships that influence others, has sold more than 45,000 copies and has been #1 in four business categories.

He's been a featured guest on 500+ podcasts, radio and TV shows, and has been regular FOX News radio contributor.

Jason has his law degree and masters in communications from Syracuse University.

You can find more about his specialized coaching options (with individuals and organizations), products, books and more at JasonTreu.com

Thank you for purchasing the book.

I really appreciate all your feedback, and I love hearing what you have to say...along with the challenges you are facing and successes you are creating.

PLEASE leave a review on Amazon.
I really appreciate this because the number of reviews have a major influence on the success of a book.